The Social Context of

Economic Behavior

MODERN MANAGEMENT SERIES

G. Jay Anyon MANAGING AN INTEGRATED PURCHASING PROCESS

John Fayerweather FACTS AND FALLACIES OF INTERNATIONAL BUSINESS

Myron Heidingsfield and Frank H. Eby, Jr. MARKETING AND BUSINESS RESEARCH

Thomas Moranian THE RESEARCH AND DEVELOPMENT ENGINEER AS MANAGER

Richard D. Robinson INTERNATIONAL BUSINESS POLICY

Edward B. Shils AUTOMATION AND INDUSTRIAL RELATIONS

W. T. Tucker THE SOCIAL CONTEXT OF ECONOMIC BEHAVIOR

The Social Context of
Economic Behavior

▶ ▶ ▶ ▶ ▶ ▶ ▶ ▶ ▶ ▶ ▶ ▶ ▶ ▶ ▶ ▶ ▶ ▶ ▶ ▶

W. T. TUCKER
THE UNIVERSITY OF TEXAS

HOLT, RINEHART AND WINSTON, INC.

NEW YORK • CHICAGO • SAN FRANCISCO • TORONTO • LONDON

330.19
T 895

Library of Congress Catalog Card Number: 64-12733
28547-0114
Printed in the United States of America

For Aunt Kay and Uncle Paul

WHOSE DIVERSE VIEWS ON ECONOMIC MATTERS HAVE
SERVED AS A CONSTANT SOURCE OF STIMULATION.

Acknowledgments

It takes the help of a surprisingly large number of people to write even a brief and relatively simple book. Many of the examples of particular economic decisions contained here come from friends, acquaintances, and cooperative strangers whom I badgered unmercifully. For a full month I questioned my son, Jeffrey, about his work in the tobacco fields near Lake Congamond, where he held his first job, about matters that seemed to him either obvious or of no conceivable interest. Physicians, real estate agents, salesmen, and engineers patiently explained the details of both simple and complex activities. While I have tried to report faithfully the information they shared, it seems unlikely that I have always succeeded.

Accuracy in reporting is of minor importance unless it is coupled with satisfactory analysis. There my help has been of the best. Colleagues such as Ivan Belknap, Ralph Day, Forrest Hill, David Townsend, and C. P. Blair have provided me with better advice than I always chose to take. And graduate students such as James Stafford, Peter Bennett, and James McNeal have argued their points of view with partial success. Any faults of the volume are largely caused by my own stubborn refusal to regard them as faults.

Austin, Texas   W.T.T.
November 1963

Contents

ACKNOWLEDGMENTS   vii

INTRODUCTION   1

1 . . THE NATURE OF ECONOMIC EVENTS   4

2 . . CLASS, GROUP, AND CULTURE   14

3 . . THE VARIETY OF ECONOMIC DECISIONS   25

4 . . THE CONSUMER   28

5 . . WORK   50

6 . . THE SALE   69

7 . . THE NATURE OF THE BUSINESS ORGANIZATION   93

8 . . THE ADVERTISING APPROPRIATION: AN ORGANIZATIONAL DECISION   114

9 . . INTERNATIONAL BUSINESS   125

10 . . COMMUNITY ECONOMIC DEVELOPMENT   136

11 . . CONCLUSIONS: A THEORETICAL NOTE   150

REFERENCES   157

INDEX   161

Introduction

This small volume is concerned with the problem of analyzing economic events. It takes as its focus the single decision by a consumer, a worker, a firm, or a community, because it is my conviction that we often generalize about these decisions in inherently dangerous ways. Such generalizations are common among students of business and economics, who are prone to make the simplifying assumptions required by rigorous economic theory without fully realizing that they have made them. Often it is true of businessmen, who should know better but who abandon their own knowledge of affairs to accept the protocols of economics as a value system. Sometimes it is true of economists themselves who, having discovered a particular nicety of relations within the theoretical structures they have developed, are ready to prescribe cures for the world's ills.

There is nothing particularly novel in the material of this book. It merely uses the conceptual framework of sociology to discuss and to analyze individual economic decisions of various sorts. Many of these analyses come directly from sociological studies not primarily concerned with economic activities. Some come from students of business or labor problems or human relations or international trade who have either used social constructs themselves or who have talked about specific events in such detail that it is not difficult to suggest the social realities that provide the context of decision. Some of the events discussed are the result of personal interviewing and research directed toward the understanding of particular economic decisions. In sum, they may provide a background of information indicating the ways in which we oversimplify economic activities. The analytic constructs may suggest richer and more adequate views of economic behavior or economic goals.

Having said this, I must immediately make it clear that I do not believe economists to be simple-minded and that I fully recognize the extent to which even the classical and neoclassical thinkers (Adam Smith or Alfred Marshall, for instance) were more than routinely aware of the problems involved in attempting to describe human behavior in terms of economic theory. Further, it is clear that there is little agreement over what is or what is not economic theory. When I speak of economic theory in this volume, I am always referring to the hard central core of economic thinking that can be expressed in essentially mathematical terms and to the assumptions underlying that core. Price theory, macroanalytic models (whether classical or Keynesian), traditional theory of the firm, and the like are what I call here economic theory.[1] Schumpeter's notions of innovation, Veblen's instinct of workmanship, J. M. Clark's concepts of balance, Galbraith's didactics, I refuse to include — although it is the richness of vision provided by such discussions that often makes the thin and precise theoretical structures of the central core palatable.

I would plead that a healthy understanding of economic events is currently most important, not because we are at a more impressively dangerous choice point than ever before (mankind seems destined to be forever passing through eras that can easily be described as the most critical of human history) but because this one includes the strong possibility of naive and ruinous central economic policies. These are much less likely, of course, in the United States or other Western nations than in the underdeveloped countries, to which an incompatible body of economic theory may be applied. But even at home the piecemeal thinking about measures to promote economic growth or equity often seems based on fanciful assumptions about the nature of the firm or the consumer or the wage earner and their economic behavior.

No real *rapprochement* between economic theory and social theory is offered here, since their fundamental characteristics are, at this point in time, incompatible. That is, to accept either is to deny the ultimate validity of the other. The situational analysis of sociology is not only different from price theory; it is an implicit denial of the

---

[1]The student of economics will recognize that my reference is to theory as discussed in such works as G. J. Stigler, *The Theory of Price* (rev. ed.), New York, Macmillan, 1952; J. S. Bain, *Pricing, Distribution and Employment*, New York, Holt, 1953; J. F. Due and R. W. Clower, *Intermediate Economic Analysis* (ed. 4), Homewood, Ill., Irwin, 1961.

assumptions upon which price theory is based. This does not mean that one body of theory is right and the other is wrong, of course. What it suggests is that both are incomplete, partial, suspect. It seems to me that in just this set of circumstances the student should be encouraged to consider both points of view. But the approach in colleges and universities is normally such that the young scholar is forced to choose and to cleave unwaveringly to the discipline of his choice. Often the faculty sets the example of parochialism, arguing vehemently about which set of half-truths is correct — or worse, refusing to consider that such argument is even worth entering into.

This book is intended primarily for those persons who are interested in economics and business affairs and who have some knowledge of the rudiments of economic theory but little social theory. For those who also have experience in the world of affairs it will offer few surprises — although it may provide an additional framework for analysis. Perhaps it is also of some use to the young sociologist, if it can persuade him that in economic events there is an entire class of human behavior, both rich and consequential, that social theory tends to ignore or treats with casual interest.

Perhaps this introduction seems to promise much. If so, I should hasten to correct the impression. The purpose is merely to show that economic decisions do have a large social content and to suggest that until we understand the nature of that social content more adequately than we do now we cannot predict or explain economic behavior — or indulge in economic planning with any great complaisance.

1 ▶
The Nature of Economic Events

No behavior is simply economic. In every transaction people deal in more than dollars and products. A can of beans does not cost $.19; it costs $.19 plus or minus something. There is no word for the extra something that is negotiated in every sale. Sometimes what is negotiated is incremental amounts of status, or prestige or power or self-esteem. Sometimes what is negotiated is as subtle as meanings or attitudes or values. And there is no single term that will satisfactorily refer to all these forms of social currency.

To refer to this something as social energy is wrongheaded, since metaphors from the physical sciences are always dangerous when used in relationship to human activities. But for the purposes of this chapter the word will be put to such suspect use in order to refer in some general way to the noneconomic consequences and influences that inhere in all economic decisions. Perhaps an example of a simple transaction, such as that of a woman buying a $.19 can of beans, may show some of the advantages and disadvantages of the terminology.

Typically, a woman buying a can of beans picks it off the shelf and places it in her cart. She is prepared to unload it and pay for it at the check-out stand, haul it home, place it on the pantry shelf, and ultimately open it and give it to her family. But this is not all she is prepared for. She is also prepared to have people watch her carry out these activities. She gives both the beans and the price her public approval. Any passer-by is free to think that she has made a mistake in buying beans that are really no better than the $.17 brand and that she is therefore a wasteful and impractical housewife. Anyone is free to think, or even to say, that the particular brand she has bought is really quite tasteless, of nothing like the value that another brand has. A third person may comment to herself that it is foolish

4

to buy a single can of beans for $.19 when one can get two cans for $.37. Or a passing purchaser may be moved to pick up a can, since the woman in our example has expressed her faith in the product.

The cashier at the check-out counter can draw her own conclusions about the way the woman feeds her family and how well she knows food. The boy who sacks the groceries is free to approve or disapprove, to feel superior or to envy behind his smiling mask. And ultimately her own family, both husband and children, will let her know whether she has properly watched out for their interests in the matter.

In the process, not only the woman herself but those who observe her may be influenced. Any of the persons involved may be affected in three ways: she may change her opinions of other persons involved in the activity, she may change her opinion of the beans, or she may change her opinion of herself.

Imagine that the series of events takes place as follows: Mrs. A, a strikingly handsome woman of fifty, dressed immaculately, picks up the can of beans. She is observed by Mrs. B, a young housewife with a considerable knowledge of nutrition. Mrs. B cannot prevent a look of puzzlement and scorn from crossing her face, since she firmly believes that canning removes most of the vitamins from vegetables. Mrs. A notices the look. The social energy brought into play may have the following effects: Mrs. A decides that Mrs. B has extremely poor manners and is not at all the sort of person one would like to know. At the same time she may ask herself, "I wonder why she was so surprised at my picking up these beans? They are really quite good." But even as she says this to herself the beans may have lost some value in her estimation, and she may briefly wonder whether she is doing as good a job of feeding her husband as she did before the children left home. These fleeting impressions have consequences as important as the financial transactions involved. Mrs. A may be much less likely to buy that particular brand of canned beans or any other brand of canned beans in the future, because they actually cost her $.19 plus some undetermined amount of self-respect or some undetermined amount of respect from others. If her husband complains even mildly when the beans are served, the additional costs may become quite high.

Perhaps this brief description of some of the social possibilities that lie in the purchase of a can of beans sounds extreme. If so, it may be valuable to recall the first time you made a purchase of cigarettes or bought groceries for your mother or looked for a sweater for yourself. In all probability you can recall the amount of concern you had over the proper terminology to use, the fear to ask questions that would reveal your ignorance, the desire to appear to be a practiced buyer. (The first drink I ever bought at a bar was an old fashioned. That was the only drink I could think of under pressure.) Perhaps you can remember feeling distinctly uncomfortable when your mother complained about the price of sirloin or your father discussed a restaurant check with the waiter. Or perhaps you can recall the pleasure you received when a salesperson was visibly impressed by a purchase you made or your knowledge of a product.

In all these transactions something happened in addition to the exchange of merchandise for money. Yet what happened was not merely an increase or decrease in the purchaser's status. Sometimes others were influenced to buy a product they had not thought of before, or it may have been the product itself that seemed to take on new meanings, to become more dashing or more pedestrian, less valuable or more appealing. It is hard to sum up all these potential and actual changes of status or prestige, for usually no real change in the status of any individual is involved — whatever the fears or hopes of the adolescent. Rather, the diverse changes have so little in common with one another that they can hardly be subsumed under a term that is even moderately specific. That they all exist suggests the analogy to a flow of energy that may reach different objects and make one cold, another hot, and a third glow. Social energies of this sort can affect status, but they may merely affect attitudes or change opinions, slightly alter roles or influence meanings. Any of these changes may be more important in the total transaction than the merchandise or money that changes hands.

It is worth pointing out that the discussion has been focused on the simplest, most usual kinds of economic behavior: the purchases of ordinary products by ordinary people with little at stake in the matter. If any kind of economic decision could be free of social influence, certainly it should be these relatively inconsequential ones. In larger decisions — the location of a plant, the merger of corporations, the purchase of heavy equipment — not only the amounts of money involved but the amounts of social energy increase greatly. A salesman can lose his job (jobs always imply status) or win accolades over a single sale. In England commercial success may be followed by knighthood; here it is more likely to result in ambassadorial status or political candidacy. No businessman is unaware of the social consequences of his economic activities.

The important consideration at this point is that a separation of the social and economic forces that influence behavior or a failure to comprehend both social and economic goals makes it difficult to predict what people will do and equally difficult to understand just what it is that they have done in the course of business and economic transactions. A synthesis of the disciplines of sociology and economics is not currently possible, but the viewpoints of both occasionally run parallel and become subject to ready comparison. Perhaps a sound first step in such a comparison of their viewpoints with regard to economic decisions is a consideration of the approach each takes to motivation.

Motivation

Neither sociology nor economics gives major attention to the problem of motivation. But both have rather clear assumptions about the nature of human behavior. The largely parallel views that each subject takes of motivation should be fairly clearly understood in order to see their relationship. Economics and sociology generally approach motivation from the standpoint of goals and the instrumentalities used to reach these goals. Neither is particularly interested in stimuli or internal states, which are the areas that physiologists, psychologists, and social psychologists are likely to emphasize. This is not to say that sociologists or economists are unaware as individuals of the important motivational and cognitive concepts developed by the other behavioral sciences. Rather they seem to feel that by concentrating on the ways in which people attempt to reach goals it is possible to learn a great deal about human behavior. Such a viewpoint can be extremely useful, especially when the subject of motivation is itself in relative turmoil.[1]

Since the economic notions of motivation are by far the simpler, it is convenient to start with them. Economics has little concern with personal goals or individual behavior save as they influence economic aggregates that relate to the growth or stability of the economic system itself or rather large subdivisions of it. These aggregates

[1]A symptom of this turmoil can be seen in "Man's Construction of His Alternatives," in *The Assessment of Human Motives* (Gardner Lindzey, Ed.), New York, Holt, 1958. In it Kelly repudiates the entire concept of motivation.

are, of course, not thought of as immediate personal goals but as indicants of economic conditions in which the achievement of personal goals may be facilitated. Personal goals are usually considered to be hedonic or materialistic (terms such as "maximization of satisfaction" at least encourage this interpretation), and consist of or imply products or services.

Of primary importance in the acquisition of these products and services is the relative scarcity of resources that can be converted into such form. Since these resources are scarce and one cannot have everything he desires, it becomes necessary to evaluate alternatives with some care. Choices are made rationally. A steak dinner is worth $5.00 only if it delivers five times the satisfaction one might get from a $1.00 meal. The scarce resources (whether they be time or money or physical effort) are parceled out by the individual for the "best buys" or whatever will give him the greatest sum total of pleasure.

In effect, this concept is much like Zipf's principle of least effort, which states that mankind tends to organize its behavior in such a way as to expend the least total amount of effort in achieving any goal.[2] The nature of the process can be seen quite well in road maps that tend to minimize the traveling distance between any two points. To the extent that they actually fail to minimize this distance, efforts other than those of the driver were considered. For example, the road from New Haven to Westfield is less than perfectly straight in order to avoid building separate roads to Granby and Plantville and in order to avoid excessive cuts and fills. Language is an excellent object lesson in the economy of effort, according to Zipf. The more frequently a word is used, the shorter it is. Thus "I" is one of the shortest words in most languages, normally being a single syllable, such as *je* in French, *yo* in Spanish, *ich* in German, and *ya* in Russian.

One of the major consequences of this kind of thinking is the possibility of reducing the relative desirability of all goals to a single measuring device or medium of exchange such as dollars. The highest price in dollars that a person will pay for something is referred to as the value or utility of the product or service. On this basis the value of a two-hundred mile plane ride can be compared with that of a dress or a fishing rod or a pound of dried peas in realistic fashion. Given these basic concepts and an extremely limited number of assumptions about the number of buyers and sellers, the information

[2]George Kingsley Zipf, *Human Behavior and the Principle of Least Effort*, Reading, Mass., Addison-Wesley, 1949.

they have about one another's activities, and their freedom to enter or leave the market, economics has built a remarkably subtle and complex theory of economic behavior. And, while this analysis will not always permit one to predict behavior accurately, sometimes it does, and it serves the valuable function of acting as a bench mark for comparison with actual behavior.[3]

Two additional concepts are necessary to explain the motivational system implicit in most current economic thinking. Both are notions that make considerable sense. The first of these is related to the fact that the person or institution purchasing a product or service has a limited use for it. For example, it might well make sense to buy two pounds of dried peas or several dresses at the same price. It would not make much sense, however, to keep buying dresses over and above the number that one could wear or sell. A woman without a cocktail dress might feel the need for one so badly that she would pay a magnificent sum for it, if such dresses were priced at the maximum she would spend. Having one, the same woman might feel less urgent about the acquisition of a second. If necessary, she might still pay a high price (much higher than the prices at which dresses normally sell). But the greatest amount she would give for the second would probably be less than she would be willing to give for the first. The same woman with sixty-nine cocktail dresses might be unwilling to buy another at any price. Perhaps dresses are a bad example, since it is a common belief that women have an endless appetite for new clothing. On the other hand, there is little evidence that women with a great deal of money ever spend it all on clothing or all on anything else. In economic terminology the marginal utility of an additional dress falls below its asking price. At that point the purchases stop, since every transaction indicates that the value of the product is for the buyer greater than and for the seller less than the purchase price. (Of course, there are prices so precisely balanced that either buyer or seller is indifferent: equally willing to make or not make the transaction.)

While marginal analysis is an important tool to the economist, the second concept, that of satisficing, has not yet proved to be.[4] Satisficing contradicts the underlying notion that everyone attempts

---

[3]In effect, concepts of minimizing, optimizing, and combinations of maximizing and minimizing are sophisticated corollaries of this approach.

[4]For instance, J. F. Due and R. W. Clower, *Intermediate Economic Analysis* (ed. 4), Homewood, Ill., Irwin, 1961, devotes less than two pages to the concept of satisficing.

to maximize the utilities received in exchange for his scarce resources. Rather he merely tries to satisfy certain needs and wants and is likely to come away with something less than the best of all possible combinations of products and services. The same holds for economic institutions, such as companies that are thought to settle for a satisfactory profit rather than rigorously attempting to get the greatest profit possible.

Other social scientists occasionally poke fun at the simplicity of the economist's motivational concepts without acknowledging the remarkable power these few notions have to explain certain characteristics of all human behavior rather than merely economic activities. The person who plays tennis must make a choice between that and other activities as a way of spending his scarce resources of time and energy. And after two or three sets he quits because the marginal utility of another set will cost more in terms of those resources than it will return in pleasure. As one economist remarked, "The marginal utility of a third drink is not the same for all people."

Despite its parsimony, logical coherence, and strong appeal to common sense, the economist's implicit notions of human motivation are simply not satisfactory. Because they are so clear and their consequences have been worked out so thoroughly, it is now obvious that they do not provide an adequate model of economic activities. Quite often things that they predict do not happen and things that they cannot predict do.

Of course, it would be foolish to suggest that economic theory should be cast out simply because it is a less than perfect predictor of what people, in sum, will do in given circumstances. Social theory really has not any better record when it comes to predicting, but it does explain a good number of the reasons why economic theory falls down.

Social theory is superficially compatible with economic theory because the two take much the same view of motivation. Both emphasize the things people are trying to get rather than trying to explain why they want them. And both spend most of their effort on the ways in which people go about reaching their objects or trying to reach them.

But the world of the sociologist is very different from that of the economist. It is only a minor oversimplification to say that the economist's world is one of selfishness and competition while the sociologist's is one in which the goals of the individual are derived from social goals and in which competition is less usual than cooperation. The child learns that the best way to maximize pleasure (or even to satisfy demands for it) is to please the rest of the family. He gets a football by buttering up Dad or by passing all his subjects in school (a mildly competitive exercise where success really depends upon cooperating with the teacher). And the truth is that he only wants a football because everyone has been telling him for years that he has to want one. In the early chapters of *Social Organization* Cooley gives a most persuasive account of the way in which the infant discovers that all goals are reached through social approval and cooperation, first of the family and then of other groups.[5] Pleasing the social groups one is a member of becomes the general goal through which one achieves particular goals. Further, the particular goals themselves are often merely things society has taught the individual to want. Even under pressure of the most primitive bodily urges, he selects his own society's means of satisfying them. The young American gets hungry for a hamburger rather than for dried shrimp or a tortilla.

To this point the concepts of sociology and economics fit neatly together. The individual learns to please other people because this maximizes his scarce resources, then he expends his scarce resources in such a way as to maximize his satisfactions. Of course, many of his satisfactions will entail the satisfaction of others since he must operate within the social context. By purchasing an automobile, he adds to the scarce resources of a salesman, an automobile dealer, and thousands of workers and stockholders. By going to a movie, he adds to the scarce resources of a Sophia Loren.

The economist and sociologist might combine to state that wealth and social approval really become the major goals of all civilized people, since both can be translated into any specific, immediate objective. In fact, it should be noted that either can be converted into the other with a minimum of ingenuity and effort. They might be looked at as nearly synonymous goals, since the achievement of one without the other is rather less common than one might imagine.

The difficulty in dealing with these concepts in this relatively simple fashion is that social approval is not a particularly precise notion. Much depends on who approves and in what way they approve, what powers their approval confers, and what they demand in day-to-day repayment for that approval. The approval of society is seldom universal or automatically continued. In a way it is earned

[5]Charles Horton Cooley, *Social Organization*, New York, Scribner, 1909.

in much the same sense that money is earned (or inherited, of course, with a rather interesting social tax levied in the process so that the son cannot claim all his father's prestige or power any more than he can claim all his estate). And it can be squandered or spent in much the same way that money can, since both are media of exchange.

Social approval is usually referred to as status, caste, prestige, popularity, power, or something of the sort. The nuances are important, since status implies a kind of functional power that popularity does not. But all these forms of social approval are related to some sort of power or ability to get people to do things. A Roger Maris may have the kind of social approval that can pack the Yankee Stadium, but he probably could not get many people to switch their votes in a national election or use his particular variety of renown to get an investor to buy New York Central bonds. Of course, on the other hand, if the editor of the *Wall Street Journal* were to play right field for the Yankees, his presence would probably sell as few tickets as he would hit home runs. In society the individual's function or role has much to do with the kinds of power he has. The actual amount of power may, of course, differ widely for individuals with the same role.

But the sources of power remain always the same: people. People who admire, fear, hate, love, or envy create the essential energies of society by their numbers and the intensity of their emotion. And power is, like economic wealth, unevenly held. Some members of society have much more than others. Unlike money, these social energies cannot be placed in a bank to draw interest. Unused, they evaporate slowly. But adventitiously used they grow, sometimes at a fantastic rate. Carelessly used, they depreciate, often more rapidly than they can be converted into action or money or any of the other things they can normally buy. Tommy Manville exhausted his inherited power years before he could seriously dent his inherited wealth, and has been forced to convert dollars into social power at an increasing rate.

This flow of social energy that can be collected (or better, focused) as power by any individual can be conferred by a few people with considerable power of their own or by many with lesser power. In all human transactions, including economic ones, there is some flow of social energy. And, since it can be converted into money — is in many ways identical with money — it will necessarily affect all economic behavior and every economic decision. The effect may be great or small depending upon the magnitudes and directions of flow as sensed by the participants.

The sensing of the flow of social energy is very different from reading a balance sheet or taking physical inventory. There can be no precise accounting for social energy. But that is not to say that it cannot be approximated. The whole art of public relations is concerned with the development and measurement of limited sorts of social energy: the sorts that relate to public attitudes and opinions. And anyone with a minimum of intelligence can anticipate reasonably well the way an act will influence his intimate acquaintances. In fact, such a judgment of social consequences is so normal, so frequently carried out by everyone, that the process is often automatic or subconscious. What we find objectionable in Dale Carnegie or Machiavelli is the careful consideration of those consequences. We would rather take the accountant's approach to the problem and sum up all the social power that a giant corporation can muster, refer to it as good will, and value it at one dollar.

To understand why this accounting for the flow of social energy should be largely subconscious, how it can be reasonably accurately measured, and why it should be given such low financial regard by the accountant, we must look at the major constructs of sociology: class, group, and culture.

2 ▶

Class, Group, and Culture

The three principal sociological structures that influence individual behavior are class, group, and culture. Each is complex enough to require some explanation before it is possible to relate it to business decisions and economic behavior.

Class

There is probably no such thing as a classless society of any size. But the discernment of what the various classes are and of who belongs to which is extremely difficult in the modern world. Nowhere is the clear line of demarcation that separated nobility from yeomanry in the middle ages currently available. Nowhere is the distinction between freeman and slave as rigorously applied today as it was in Rome at the height of its power or in the United States a little more than a hundred years ago. For that reason some persons dislike using the term "class" with its implication of major, continuing social divisions when discussing contemporary United States society. But all hierarchic differences are not simply degrees along some continuum. Even in our relatively mobile society there are barriers to mobility. And crossing one of these ill-defined barriers is a very different thing from the acquisition of a bit more prestige or status or power.

In all parts of the world people can and do move from one class to another, although the restrictions on such movements differ greatly from one society to another. The result is that no one really knows how many classes there are in any particular society, and even in a highly class-conscious area such as England, it becomes necessary for

14

Nancy Mitford to explain with some humor how one can tell persons of one class from those of another. In a supposedly un-class-conscious United States, *Life* magazine finds it expeditious to discuss with some humor the differences among the highbrow, the middlebrow, and the lowbrow. The fact that these popular attempts to explain class are so often humorous merely emphasizes the serious regard most people have for the subject.

There have been many efforts to describe social class in this country in a scholarly way. The numerous studies of particular cities, towns, and areas make it clear that a given locale may have a relatively small or a relatively large number of class divisions and that the criteria of class may vary considerably.[1] While there is considerable temptation to deal with the academic subtleties, doubts, and alternative analyses in the manner of Robin Williams, the purposes of this volume are better served by the simpler and more direct Warner classification.[2] Warner's concept of an essentially six-class society is one of the few that has both extensive empirical support and a reliable methodology for the determination of an individual's class.[3] His principal criteria of class relate to income, source of income, education, occupation, and neighborhood. Table 1 gives a list of the classes and a rough suggestion of the kinds of persons they contain.

The perception of social class is quite different from the reality of social class. When asked, people have a strong tendency to say they are middle class no matter what class they belong to. Barry Goldwater, if asked, would probably tell you that he belonged to the middle class; so would many a subsistence farmer in northern Georgia. In all probability both would mean what they said. At the same time, people are prone to draw extremely artificial distinctions (even more artificial than any of those suggested above) between themselves and others. Some medical doctors make it clear that they regard dentists as belonging to a lower class than that of the M. D. Presi-

[1]See W. Lloyd Warner and Paul S. Lunt, *The Status System of a Modern Community*, Vol. II, Yankee City Series, New Haven, Yale University Press, 1942; John Dollard, *Caste and Class in a Southern Town* (ed. 2), New York, Harper, 1949; James West, *Plainville, U.S.A.*, New York, Columbia University Press, 1945; Robert S. and Helen M. Lynd, *Middletown: A Study in Contemporary American Culture*, New York: Harcourt, Brace, 1929, as a few of the classic studies.

[2]See Robin M. Williams, Jr., *American Society, A Sociological Interpretation* (ed. 2), New York, Knopf, 1960, pp. 87–138.

[3]W. Lloyd Warner, M. Meeker, and K. Eells, *Social Class in America*, Chicago, Science Research Associates, 1949.

TABLE 1

Class	Description
Upper Upper	Families with old wealth: certainly Henry Cabot Lodge, probably Henry Ford II, possibly Jack Kennedy prior to election
Lower Upper	Old families with declining wealth, the newer wealthy, some persons with prestigious jobs: J. Paul Getty, Sam Goldwyn, Barry Goldwater, possibly the local millionaire
Upper Middle	Well off, well educated with respected job or profession: the doctor, the bank officer, the corporation executive, the newspaper editor
Lower Middle	Salaried, probably high-school education: the proprietor of the small store, the clerical worker, the supervisor, the fireman
Upper Lower	The hourly wage earner, grammar-school education: the retail sales clerk, the carpenter, the small farmer
Lower Lower	Little education, irregular job: the migrant laborer, the small tenant farmer, the slum dweller

dents of $400,000,000 banks are apt to feel vastly superior to those of $130,000,000 banks, who feel, in turn, superior to the presidents of $60,000,000 banks. Sales clerks in Neiman Marcus must often look down on the public accountants and oil millionaires they wait on.

Since membership in a social class is not determined by commonly accepted criteria, as it was in feudal societies, and, since it is obvious that people do move from one to another, it is not difficult for any individual or group to develop its own specious criteria of class. Thus, it becomes possible for the artist and the businessman to look down on one another, the one holding that creative achievement is the real measure of a man, the other equally certain that income is the valid measure.

In this process of derogating someone else's position the *social* character of social class is often lost sight of. Moral class or intellectual class or financial class or celebrity may become the basis of judgment. Socially, Washington was upper class, Jackson was lower class, and Wilson was middle class. Socially, Caligula was upper class and St. Peter was lower class.

A great many people are difficult to classify because of their social mobility or because of pseudo-class distinctions. Among the persons hardest to locate in a class are the celebrities. The famous actor, the boxing champion, the Olympic dash man, the comic-strip creator, the novelist: all defy classification. One day they may be working as busboys, the next day they may be dined by the mighty, on the third they may sleep in a flop house. Seldom do celebrities wield social power greater than that common to the middle classes, although they may be accepted as companions by the upper class. In effect, they seem to lose what real class they had and fall into a pseudo-class that is no more functional than the key to the city, the honorary Kentucky colonelship, or the title of Miss Nuts and Bolts of 1962.

Another type of pseudo-class is extremely important to the functioning of most institutions. This might be referred to as rank, since its distinction from social class is most readily observable in military organization. The lines drawn between ranks are meticulous and highly functional. They are analogous to social class; in fact, military rank was, in times past, an almost perfect reflection of social class and is currently related to it. But rank can run counter to class. An upper-class private may serve under a lower-class captain, although this is not the usual order of affairs. So also in other institutions, such as corporations and colleges, churches and government, the social realities of class may be reversed by the operational requirements of rank. Both social class and institutional rank are real and functional. In addition they are tremendously important to people. It is therefore not easy for the upper-class private to take orders from the lower-class captain or for the upper-middle-class bookkeeper to take direction from the lower-middle-class office manager. And it is no easier for the captain and the office manager to be fair-minded and effective superiors in situations of this sort.

The economic consequences and appurtenances of both class and pseudo-class are not difficult to find. Salesmen have taken lower-paying jobs to get prestigious titles. Men have been turned down for jobs they were capable of handling because their table manners or speech gave their social class away. Taste in home décor and dress and food is related to class as much as to income. The young, upper-middle-class couple and the young, lower-middle-class couple with the same income usually spend their money quite differently.

The full effects of class and pseudo-class can only be explained, however, in connection with the individual's attitude toward class. Not everyone has the same hopes and fears regarding his position in society. It is popular to emphasize the struggle up the social ladder or the fall down it. But the one is not a particularly common hope nor the other a particularly common fear. In all probability most people are principally concerned with maintaining their current social position. To rise even a moderate distance in the class structure may be as frightening a possibility as that of a long downward fall. Small incremental movements in an upward direction are acceptable, perhaps even expected, but these amount to changes in status, prestige, or power rather than shifts from one class to another. And they are not sought with vigor except by the uncommon individual.

But almost universal are the fear of encroachment on one's social position by members of a lower class and the fear of slipping just a bit down the ladder. Minimal changes in *relative* position are often viewed as matters of vital concern. The management trainee learns that his superiors do not want him to drive a better car than they do even if he can afford it. The upper-middle-class country club turns down the successful plumber's application for membership. Some companies have as many as fifteen distinct hourly wage levels relating to pseudo-class ranks below the salaried employee level. A raise in the wage rate of one requires an adjustment of all the others. In fact, in business pseudo-class has become so important that the relative size of salaries among administrators is at least as important as their absolute level, since differences in salaries are perceived as differences in standing or class. A part of the resistance to Negroes' moving into a neighborhood is related to the fear of loss of social position. And when persons of slightly lower status begin purchasing mink coats and Cadillacs, these former class symbols may actually be avoided by those who previously regarded them as the hallmarks of high social standing.

Group

While membership in a class is impersonal and often inaccurately perceived, group membership may be obvious and intimate. In fact, the degree of intimacy is an important variable in the classification of groups. Primary groups are closely knit, small, intimate groups, such as the primitive family. Of course, many families today are primary groups although their bonds are probably less tight than those of families in former periods. Secondary groups, such as a neighborhood, are, by contrast, larger and less interdependent. But they are still characterized by face-to-face contact, reasonably close personal acquaintance, and a complex of common goals. It is clear that just as all families are not primary groups, so all neighborhoods are not secondary groups. In sociology much attention has been given to the deterioration of the traditional primary and secondary groups. The great metropolitan society seemed to breed fewer loyalties and common values than the earlier primary and secondary groups. In truth the nature of groups was merely changing and much of the social energy was still generated in informal organizations very like the traditional primary and secondary groups.

There is no easy classification of groups at present. The degree of intimacy remains an important consideration. The degree of formality does also, although it seems an oversimplification to regard groups as simply formal or informal. None the less, these dichotomous terms will have to be used on occasion because of the relatively informal social organization that grows within formal organizations.

In general the course of events is from informal organization to formal organization to institution. An informal organization could be thought of as a group of people who occasionally get together and discuss matters of common interest. When they elect a president and a secretary-treasurer and meet every Tuesday at 9:00 P.M. they become a formal organization. When they become Kiwanis, International, or the Society for the Preservation and Encouragement of Barber Shop Singing in America, International, they can be considered institutions.[4] And by that time they will contain within their ranks new and subtle informal organizations.

It will be necessary to mention peer groups, work groups, interest groups, reference groups, ethnic groups, and others from time to time because they are useful concepts, but there is no general rule about what kinds of groups have to be considered in sociological analysis.

The importance of the group lies in its influence on the attitudes and opinions of the individual and its creation of much of the immediate context within which decisions of all sorts are made.[5] Diffi-

[4]The term "institution" is used to indicate something beyond and different from the contemporary organization. The Methodist-Episcopal Church has both an organizational and an institutional character. The ladies' afternoon bridge club is an American institution, but an individual bridge club of this sort is only a formal or informal organization whose success or failure is but distantly related to that of the social institution.

[5]See Richard LaPiere, *A Theory of Social Control*, New York, McGraw-Hill, 1954, pp. 99–129.

culties in determining what the nature of the influence or the context will be in a given situation are largely founded on the fact that an individual usually belongs to several groups, sometimes to a large number of them. It may be quite difficult to determine in advance what the various directions and strengths of his many group loyalties will be.

The young executive of a corporation belongs to many formal and informal groups. Let us imagine for a moment the situation of Peter Brown of Stamford, Connecticut. He has a family, a wife and two children, as his central primary group. He has a group of intimates who commute with him to New York. Two of this group often meet him at the Commodore bar before train time in the evening. With some regularity he plays golf with one of these and five or six other club members. At the office there are four or five on his product management team who lunch together and fight out the corporate skirmishes side by side. Then there are a few college chums with whom he occasionally meets for an evening in town; one of these he would refer to as his best friend. Each of these groups or quasi-groups commands a certain amount of his loyalty.

Then there are a number of formal groups and institutions to which he belongs. He is nominally a member of the P. T. A. but attends only a few of the evening meetings. He belongs to the Presbyterian church and the Glenview golf club. He is a member of the American Marketing Association and the Sales Executives' Club. He is a class secretary in his college alumni association. And he is, of course, an employee of the BBB corporation.

This is a modest series of group relationships for a twentieth-century American to maintain. But even a number this large would not be possible if it were not for the fact that most of these groups and institutions have modified their demands to suit those of other groups and to accommodate a reasonable number of individual differences. The minister does not become irate when Peter Brown plays golf on Sunday morning. He even tolerates those members who show up for service only once or twice a year. His fellow commuters will not throw Peter Brown off the train or even refuse to sit with him if he reads the *Daily News* rather than the *Times* or *Tribune* — although they will probably lower him a bit in their estimation. Further, the mere fact that he commutes to work means that some of these groups and institutions are unaware of large portions of his activities. He may lose his job, keep taking his regular train to the city as he looks for another, and maintain respect as a business executive until he finds another position. If he moves rapidly, it may be that he can keep all the nonwork groups with which he is associated — even his family — unaware of the unpleasant problem until he has solved it.

Lastly, all the groups he belongs to have pretty much the same general sets of values. He is unlikely to please any one group immensely and at the same time offend another seriously. While it would be pretentious to attempt to list even the major values of these groups, it is none the less clear that business success is an important value to all of them, while the ability to carry a tune is important in almost none.

But to point out the extent to which these groups have adapted to one another, are insulated from one another, and even have much the same systems of values is not to deny the real conflicts among them or the diverse influences they exert. In none of his economic decisions, personal or corporate, can Peter Brown escape his group loyalties or his group-formed values. If he buys a hat, it will be one approved (or at least tolerated) by the groups in whose presence he intends to wear it. If he is offered a promotion that will send him to a regional office in Atlanta, his acceptance or rejection of the new job will largely depend upon the reactions of various groups and his loyalty to them. When he hires an assistant, his college friends or fellow commuters may be persuasive in getting him to tip the scales a bit in favor of a particular applicant. More probably he does not consciously tip the scales any more than he consciously attempts to please some group in buying a hat. In both cases he is most likely to please himself, to use his own judgment and his own taste — not realizing, or only partially realizing, the extent to which that taste and judgment are products of the forces exerted on him by his interactions with various groups.

To understand the nature of decisions some account must be taken of groups the individual does not belong to as well as those he does. Intergroup tensions become major sources of social influence. Peter Brown may approve an expenditure by the Glenview golf club largely because he wants it to be more impressive than the Fairfield country club. He may fight against the point of view of the comptroller of BBB corporation and regard it as a victory for his product team against hostile forces when he wins. The very existence of groups indicates a we–they way of thinking that is normal to most circumstances and of major importance in business, since it may affect the objectives of a company or industry just as it does those of other social groups and institutions.[6]

Culture

As the foregoing discussion has shown, the concepts of class and group are not completely discrete. Groups tend to form within classes, but larger groups and institutions may include several classes. And, of course, a class always includes a vast number of groups. It is not surprising, then, that a group boundary may be contiguous with a class boundary and that group interactions may readily be mistaken for class interactions or vice versa. The difficulties that arise from such inexactness are not of major importance except to the professional sociologist, whose task they in part define.

In the same way, certain problems of deciding whether it is culture, class, or group that is the source of a particular social influence are implicit in any discussion of culture. Since a small, face-to-face group is usually composed of persons from the same class and the same culture, it may seem disturbing that the ultimate source of power existing in the group may largely derive from class or culture. While it does not solve the problem to point out that groups and institutions are the mechanisms by which culture is modified and passed on, and that classes are natural major divisions of society which occur in all known cultures, it may mitigate it.

The influence of culture is less obvious than that of class and much less obvious than that of group. Almost everyone is aware of group pressures, no matter how unthoughtful or untutored he is. Almost everyone is similarly aware of class distinctions, although he may be relatively unaware of the ways in which his thinking and behavior are different from those of other classes. Most of us are naive about culture. Even the adult who knows perfectly well that his eating habits are dominated by cultural patterns he has internalized does not say to himself, "I am hungry. Because I live on the North American Continent, I have learned to assuage that hunger with roast beef. If I were a native of India, the notion of eating roast beef would appall me. And if I were a person living on Jaluit, I would not think of roast beef because I would never have tasted it, heard of

[6]One of the most thorough discussions of groups, their organization and influence, is George C. Homans, *The Human Group*, New York, Harcourt Brace, 1950.

it, or seen it." He merely says, "I am hungry for prime ribs." Obviously, it would be impossible to consider one's cultural inheritance every time a decision was made.

Most of our preferences are cultural preferences. Most of our values are cultural values. Most of our customs are cultural. The reason why this is not continually apparent may be that we are so involved in perceiving and reacting to the differences between people and the differences between highly similar groups that we see little value in drawing distinctions between Americans and Samoans. It is much more important in day-to-day living to understand the differences between good credit risks and poor credit risks, capable salesmen and mediocre salesmen, prospectively acceptable mates and unacceptable ones. What they have in common (culture) is simply too common to be useful for most purposes.

Of course, culture is not static. Especially in our time cultural change is comparatively rapid. But a rapid cultural change is unbelievably slow. It took women eighty years to get the right to vote after they first began to press for that reform. Today, the excitement, the threats of catastrophe, the promises of utopia that attended that long effort seem ridiculous. It is hard to understand why women should have fought so hard for the right or why men should have denied it to them for so long (or thrown them in prison for making speeches about the matter).

Culture is, naturally, a major influence in economic decisions, since it not only forms the broad base of the value system but also provides a misleading account of human nature. When someone makes an economic decision, he often bases it on his concept of human nature. And often he makes the mistake of thinking, "This is what people are like," rather than "This is what people are like now in this culture." The result is that large, conservative corporate interests often miss the major economic opportunities of the period. It is not by chance that the automotive industry grew from isolated, individual shops. The major corporations of the period knew that it was against human nature for people to want to go whizzing around faster than a horse could trot. It is not by chance that Birdseye had to work desperately for many years to develop the frozen food industry. The big food processors knew that people did not really want frozen foods and that retailers would not be interested in handling them. It is not by chance that the producers and actors and theater owners of the legitimate stage played almost no part in the development of the motion

picture industry. They knew the culture and the traditions of dra na
too well to imagine that people would pay to see shadows on a screen
rather than live actors on a stage.

Of course, many corporations today are considerably more alert
to the possibility of changes in the kinds of products people will buy.
But there are reasons to believe that they are thinking with culturally
dominated conservatism about other economic activities. For instance, our culture places a high value on youth, and, despite the
growing evidence that older persons form a ready supply of able
workers who have low absenteeism, cause few personnel problems,
and are highly productive, many firms refuse to consider them as
prospective employees. Managers of these firms often state as their
reason for not wanting older workers the fact that older workers are
often sick, quarrelsome, and hard to get along with, and are unproductive. But usually these managers have not even kept records on
their own workers by age. Any career woman can attest to the fact
that traditional (cultural) attitudes toward women in business normally cloud up economic decisions.

It would be a serious mistake to believe that corporate enterprise
is unaware of social organization and its functions. Their market
success demonstrates that they have generally adapted to their culture, used social groups effectively, and organized themselves roughly
in terms of social class. Nor is it possible to accuse economists of
ignoring the kinds of useful constructs that sociology can provide.
Veblen had begun to relate the two disciplines before the turn of the
century. And almost every first-rate economist since that time has
had a keen eye for at least some sociological phenomena. Further,
almost any intelligent observer who is willing to think concretely will
recognize the numerous interrelations between social influences and
economic behavior. This volume serves only the modest function of
attempting a somewhat more complete statement of the various social
influences on a wide range of economic decisions. In the attempt it
leans heavily on research and analysis in both disciplines, since some
of the subareas have been reasonably well worked.

3 ▶
The Variety of Economic
Decisions

In a market society like ours most events, most decisions, most activities have economic consequences or implications. Engagements announced in the society section of the local paper imply the purchase of a diamond, the selection of a flatware pattern, showers for which friends will buy gifts and refreshments, new dresses and lingerie for the bride. And it is almost certain that the engaged couple has discussed the economics of family living in detail. Decisions about whether to rent an apartment or buy a house and whether the bride will keep her job after marriage will have been made and remade a half-dozen times.

The decision to run for Congress or the Aldermanic Board must in part be an economic decision. Who will pay the printing bills or rent the auditorium? How much will it cost to furnish beef for the barbecue or advertising for the newspaper or time on the local TV station? In fact, the right to run for office must be purchased like a bag of stick candy or a driver's license. (So many candidates filed for the last gubernatorial primary in Texas that discussion of the adequacy of the $50.00 fee led to an increase in the price of what few would regard as a negotiable commodity.)

The golf match, the fishing trip, the high-school dance: all involve economic decisions and, not infrequently, economic decisions that are both numerous and consequential to the parties involved. Even turning on the TV set indicates, in effect, a willingness to pay for whatever electrical power is used and to countenance a partial destruction of the set itself. And every high-school student is briefed on the economic advantage of a college education.

It is clear, of course, that all actions and decisions of business firms are, by definition, essentially economic. It may be less common-

25

ly understood that all governmental actions are equally so, unless one is aware of the close attendance Wall Street gives to news from Washington and the major impact of government spending on the economy. It was not by accident that the first legislative act of the United States Congress was an indirect subsidy of domestic shipping.

The point that virtually all activities have economic consequences may seem trivial unless one recognizes the extent to which our economy depends upon the anticipation of consumer wants. A moderately serious overbuilding of two-bedroom homes occurred in many areas in the early 1950's because contractors did not predict the high birth rate in young families.

Quite obviously it would be foolishly single-minded to consider all decisions economic decisions simply because they have some immediate or ultimate economic consequence. On the other hand, the category of functions provided by economic thought (such as consumption, production, and investment) does not encourage the kind of situational or institutional analysis that seems required in a discussion of this sort. The result is that there is no attempt here to define just what an economic decision is. In fact, there is implicit in these pages the notion that the phrase "economic decision" is, at best, frighteningly loose terminology.

None the less, some kinds of decisions and some kinds of behavior are commonly thought of as economic. Most of these are characterized by an act of buying or selling or are directed toward purchases or sales. An individual sells his labor for salary or wages or buys products for his personal use. A corporation buys a plant and tools and labor in order to sell some product it can make with these resources. The governmental units sell their services for taxes and buy services and products with which to provide protection, education, highways, and the thousand other public services. And the primary governmental decisions directed toward moderating economic fluctuations are simply purchases and sales of claims against itself or changes in the terms of such sales and purchases.

The material in this book is generally focused on the setting and the context in which decisions to buy or sell are made. In so doing, it concentrates on what has come to be known as the private sector of the economy: the people who work, the businesses that hire them, and the managers who run those businesses. The virtual elimination of governmental activities from the discussion does not imply that governmental decisions have less than major economic consequence or that they are immune to social considerations.

Any thorough analysis of Federal Reserve Board decisions in control of monetary policy would have to recognize the odd organizational pattern that essentially isolates the Board of Governors from the technical staff. This relative isolation effectively eliminates the informal staff-board relationships normally required for the development of an effective advisory system. Close observers suggest that the Board of Governors acts not so much against the advice of its technical staff as without it, which may account in part for the Federal Reserve Board's failure to follow a consistently contracyclical policy.

The variety of decisions and situations discussed in this book is, none the less, broad; it ranges from those made by farmers in the Ozarks to those made by giant power companies or medium-sized banks, from real estate agencies in the Southwest to zoning commissions in the Northeast. The progress is generally from decisions by individuals to those by organizations. And the selection of consumer decisions as a starting point reflects a personal belief that the satisfaction of consumer wants is the ultimate measure of any economic structure.

4 ▶

The Consumer

In the folklore of the sixties consumer purchases may be classed as economic behavior only in the sense that they have economic consequences. The process by which they are made is generally granted to be both uneconomic and irrational. The consumer is reputedly obsessed, impulsive, and suggestible — driven by his subconscious and the shrewd manipulators of the market place. The housewife has even been accused of purchasing her groceries while in a semihypnotic state.[1]

Many students of consumer behavior believe that too much emphasis is currently being given to what may be going on subconsciously inside the consumer's head and that too little attention has been given to what the consumer does and the situation within which he carries out his activities. It is certain that many existing texts (most of them marketing texts) oversimplify and misapply psychological theory. There is not space here to discuss the many theoretical structures of psychology in any systematic way, despite the fact that they pertain to the genesis and evolution of wants in the individual, relate to his perceptual and cognitive processes, and concern his modes of behavior and his affective states. Yet these certainly need discussion, for to a great extent they have been ignored in the psychologizing that is common in both popular and professional publications.

While no such major undertaking is possible here, it seems necessary to note a few basic concepts about consumer behavior that

[1]The best-selling *Hidden Persuaders* by Vance Packard (New York, McKay, 1957) is but one of many publications contributing to a new folklore of consumer behavior that seriously overstates the role of subconscious processes and confuses emotion and irrationality.

underly the principal analyses of this discussion. First, it is assumed that consumer decisions are goal-seeking decisions that are relatively successful in the given situation. That is, A can probably make his own choices better than B or C or D can make them for him. Most individual decisions are reached after the weighing of a large number of factors (or the analysis of a complex situation) in a relatively informal way. Where the outcome is of no particular importance, or can be predicted with great accuracy (often this implies that the same product is frequently purchased), this informal analysis may be carried out almost instantaneously. In any case, the decision-making process is not entirely conscious. Not only are there subconscious and partly conscious goals, there are also subconscious and partly conscious evaluations and predictions. The subconscious and partly conscious goals and processes are neither more real nor more important than those that are conscious. In fact, operations at all levels of consciousness tend to be corollary or supportive. In other words, to make the best buy the consumer must somehow take account of all his own characteristics, desires, and inclinations and those of his associates: friends, family, and acquaintances. If it were not for the fact that he can calculate all the probable responses by others subconsciously, the selection of a sports jacket might prove an extremely tedious process, comparable to programming a difficult linear problem for a computer. With the normal human equipment he need merely ask himself whether he likes the jacket or not, and, miraculously, if he wants one that his father will object to, his wife admire, and his associates envy, it will come up automatically a good share of the time.

People want a great many things. No one has ever made a very satisfactory list of them. They want rest and they want excitement, they want pleasurable sensations and they want friends, they want food and they want light. It does no good whatsoever to attempt to categorize these wants as basic drives and secondary drives. It does no good (and is fancifully egocentric) to attempt to distinguish needs from wants. It is completely useless to differentiate social from psychological from physiological needs except for theoretical research purposes. And it is the height of foolishness to speak of rational wants or needs in contradistinction to emotional wants or needs. All such distinctions are based on the notion that some wants are more important than others, more proper, or more functional in all circumstances.

Any reasonably acute observer of people recognizes that there are no such things as universal needs, and that wants are relative to the situation. As a single example from the endless number that could be selected, examine the situation of the survivors of the *Lulworth Hill*, dying of starvation on the open sea. The dead were carefully rolled to the sharks, not on the presumption that it is better to be eaten by one's natural enemies than by one's friends, but simply because those who remained preferred to die as acceptable members of British society than to live as cannibals. The decision denied a so-called basic drive for a secondary drive; it refused to respond to a so-called biological need in order to obey a social dictum; it was emotional in that it was made under great stress; it was rational in that it succeeded in its purpose: the maintenance of a particular social morality.

People have wants, many diverse wants, that influence all their decisions including those that may be classed as economic. Important characteristics of these wants in relationship to economic behavior are their specificity, communality, strength, and persistence. All of these characteristics of wants are related to the social situation. The specificity of wants has considerable range. One may want a button-down, white Oxford-cloth shirt of a particular make and refuse to consider any substitute. One may want "something to eat" with a rather wide range of possible foods being acceptable. Or one may want a rewarding life without having any particularly clear notions about whether this means a new job, a divorce, a hobby, or what. Both society and business are largely responsible for the channeling of the vague, nonspecific wants into particular activities by making available a larger number of opportunities, products, and services and by providing a value system for their judgment. If one wants prestige, for instance, he may write a novel, run for elective office, buy fashionable clothing, work out with bar bells, or jump off the Brooklyn Bridge, with a reasonably accurate knowledge of what the returns in prestige will be, and what group or groups will grant that prestige.

The communality of wants is similarly bound up with social influence and business practice. Nothing demonstrates this more clearly than the fashion cycle, which requires that business develop some style that large elements of society can approve, and that society evaluate this positively. The interaction between designers and society is rather complex, since it operates through various intermediaries such as retail store buyers, fashion editors, fashion leaders, and the like. The outcome is seldom controllable, although some take the rather naive view that the garment industry makes women change their mode of dress yearly. It would be equally naive and equally true to say that consumers force the garment industry to change its designs and materials constantly. One of the interesting characteristics of the garment market is the seemingly contradictory demand that persons must wear a common style but clearly differentiated items. Apparently no woman is more ill at ease than the one who is clearly dressed out of the fashion, unless it is the one who finds another person wearing an identical garment.

It is probably not a serious overstatement to suggest that everyone wants prestige, but that only a limited number of persons want Cadillacs; that every family wants a refrigerator, but that only a limited number want twelve-foot refrigerators in violet enamel. In other words, general wants are more widespread than specific ones.

The strength of wants is often clearly related to certain social considerations, especially to the influence of the primary or face-to-face groups. The member of a Boy Scout troup may want a particular knife desperately because every other member of the troup has one, and want a tent just as desperately because no one else in the troup has one. In all probability most Americans have a hierarchy of relatively specific material wants: a new house, a camera, a pair of brown loafers, a spinning reel, a really good thick steak, and so on. The relative strength of these wants and economic circumstances will generally determine whether one refrains from eating steak in order to purchase a spinning reel or merely buys the entire lot out-of-hand and starts to construct a new list out of his more general wants.

Of course, few wants persist. Most can be satisfied for a longer or shorter period of time. Undoubtedly, the relatively specific, material wants disappear with an appropriate purchase — some may even disappear forever. Most specific wants, however, tend to be recurrent. One wants a new car after a year or two or six. One wants more ice cream after a day or week or month. The somewhat more general wants, such as that for food, recur rather more frequently than the specific, such as that for artichokes. Some few wants apparently persist with great strength over fantastically long periods. Affectional wants may inform virtually all an individual's activities over a full lifetime. Undoubtedly the most persistent wants are those essentially social wants that might be described as the desire to belong and the desire for recognition.

Almost no discussion of wants can go far without running into the means–ends problem. Are things wanted for themselves, or are they merely wanted as means to some further goal? It would be a pleasant situation if the means–ends problem could be dispensed with by the use of some clever phrase or iconoclastic argument. Unfortunately, it cannot. The teen-age girl wants a deodorant so that she will not be the source of socially unacceptable odors. She wants to smell pleasant in order to be popular with boys. She wants to be popular with boys so that someone will marry her. She wants to be married in order to participate in a normal feminine life that will include, among other things, the financial ability to buy deodorants.

The circularity is forced. Some wants are largely considered as means to an end, others are more generally thought of as ends in themselves. Unfortunately people are not particularly clear on the nature of their wants. A want that starts out as a means may become an end in itself, and one that appears to be an end may turn out, when achieved, to be merely a means to some further end. There is no satisfactory way of disposing of the problem except to suggest that all wants apparently have both means and end functions, since some people grow so enchanted with the usual means that they consider it an end in itself. Money is perhaps the article with the least sensible end function, yet it may become an ultimate goal of considerable attractive power. To suggest that a normal means is accepted as an end in itself implies that people can learn to accept substitute goals or symbolic goals. From the standpoint of popular judgment the acceptance of a symbolic goal may seem grotesque, even tragic; from the standpoint of society it is often more valuable than the achievement of an original goal. In fact, an entire romantic literature has come to surround the Schuberts, Lautrecs, and Poes — even the Arrowsmiths, Ahabs, Sammy Glicks, and Robert Jordans. Seldom is the personal satisfaction involved in the pursuit of a symbolic or substitute goal given reasonable credence, although it is a commonplace that human pleasures need not be sacral or visceral.

The foregoing may seem to be largely irrelevant to the problem of consumer behavior, or may seem to indicate that consumer behavior is surely as ridiculous as is often suggested. The purpose of including the discussion of goals is rather to suggest the richness, diversity, and subtlety of human goals. It is only natural, since man is addicted to some of the less pernicious forms of efficiency, that he should characteristically make choices that have implications both as means and as ends — and often several of each.

The bloodless critic may complain because the consumer buys a car that does not provide the most functional and economic means of transportation.[2] The consumer glories in a purchase that provides not only transportation but some measure of status, relatively luxurious physical comfort, a sense of unlimited power, a convenient place to neck, and an esthetic object of more than routine beauty. In human terms his choice is magnificent. A failure to understand this essential character of consumer behavior is so shriveled, so mechanical, that it does not even deserve healthy laughter.

None of this should be construed as suggesting that consumer choices are always perfect or even satisfactory. Always they are made with less than complete knowledge about their outcomes. Unsatisfactory choices occur. And the consumer who makes them might well quote Robert E. Lee, who when chastised by a student for the sheer stupidity of his plan of battle at Gettysburg is reputed to have said, "Even an old incompetent like me can see that now. What was needed was someone who could see it on the second of July in 1862."

While consumer choices may be made in fearful joy or lethargy, excitement or boredom, it is a serious mistake to regard them merely as goal-oriented decisions whose purposes are inscrutable. To say that things make sense only in human terms does not mean that they are beyond analysis. Economics considers the subgoals of maximizing satisfaction while minimizing expense, and sociology provides some useful concepts about the situations within which goals form and change.

Economic Subgoals

Economic goals are, for the purchasing consumer, subgoals or purchasing conditions. In buying a pair of shoes one may set a top price that can be paid and attempt to get the best pair of shoes available at that price or near it. On the other hand, one may specify informally the characteristics that the shoes should have and then attempt to get such shoes at the lowest possible price. While these are two possible general economic frames within which purchasing can take place, other combinations of minimizing, maximizing, and satisficing are not unlikely. In any case, the frame or subgoal of behaving economically is not generally adhered to with great rigor. It is mani-

---

[2]The professional economist is seldom so naive.

festly impractical for the consumer to inspect every pair of shoes in town and impossible for him to determine in advance reasonably exact measures of their comfort or longevity. He works with both incomplete and imperfect knowledge — and is quite aware of his informational shortcomings. In effect, he decides that acquiring more knowledge about the market would be more expensive in terms of time, money, and effort than the additional knowledge would be worth. Characteristically, men, who tend to value their time more highly than women, spend less of it in the purchase of comparable products.

Professor Kelley emphasizes that students of consumer purchasing have spent entirely too little time analyzing costs other than price.[3] Price itself is so difficult to calculate that it is only recently that most businesses have taken a reasonably sophisticated approach to it, formally computing the difference in value of present dollars and future dollars, for example. Consumers probably never get very specific about either price or other purchasing costs. Discount, in the form of cash, stamps, or premiums; interest charges; or delayed payment on charge accounts are probably never calculated in current cash equivalents by the consumer — although they may be approximated. Other shopping costs — time, energy, transportation, and the like — are undoubtedly important in consumer decisions (large reductions in price during gas wars will apparently bring purchasers fairly long distances, while lesser reductions seem to find consumers less willing to drive much out of their way), but they are highly unlikely to be stated by the consumer in terms of dollars and cents.

Some women apparently watch the Thursday newspaper with some care to determine where they should do their Friday grocery shopping. And some of them may make purchases at two or three different stores to take advantage of particular bargain prices. One young wife reports having compared prices on some twenty or twenty-five items in a new discount house with those in her regular supermarket. Finding them generally lower in the discount house, she began to make her weekly shopping trips there. After several weeks she discovered that her bills were almost identical with those at her regular supermarket, which was several miles closer. As a result, she switched back to her former store. She was aware that she might have purchased somewhat differently in the two stores, but dis-

[3]Eugene J. Kelley, "The Importance of Convenience in Consumer Purchasing," *Journal of Marketing*, Vol. 23, No. 1, Richard D. Irwin, Inc., Homewood, Ill., July 1958.

counted this as a factor. Her attempt to behave economically was fairly consistent, but certainly not completely accurate, simply because it is almost literally impossible to behave economically in this respect when prices and margins change with time, when week-end specials cannot be predicted, and when the value or quality of much privately branded merchandise is not completely determinable.

The important thing to note in discussing the nature of consumer purchases is that while a woman may change stores or make special trips to take advantage of certain prices, she normally does not choose the simpler method for reducing food cost — that of buying less expensive foods at any store — unless the family's financial condition becomes critical. Yet, there is little question that if one were satisfied with any well-balanced diet, the food bill for most families, even among the relatively poor, could be cut by a sizable amount. That they are not, merely says something about the relative importance of goals. Except for highly unusual people in our society, economic goals are of considerable importance without being paramount. They explain some aspects of consumer behavior moderately well, and that is an accomplishment of considerable merit. Social constructs explain other aspects of the behavior which are of equal economic importance.

Culture

The cultural anthropologist of the future who studies the twentieth century United States will find himself primarily interested in exactly the data the economists utilize now to predict and explain its economic life. Gross National Product, steel production, bank loans, box car loadings, first-class postage cancellations, automobile sales, man hours worked, per capita income, employment in the textile industry — only through the analysis of such data could the cultural anthropologist get a reasonable picture of our culture with any relative speed. In comparing 1900 and 1950, he would surely find of most interest such things as changes in income distribution, growth of the automobile industry, increases in taxes and governmental expenditures, reduction of the average work week, and the like.

All of this merely points out that business and economic activities are not only major portions of our culture, but include the data from which almost all other aspects of culture can be deduced. Those business activities that summate into economic data both influence a nation's culture and are in turn influenced by it. It would make much sense to say that the rate of economic growth is a measure of the extent to which business understands cultural values and utilizes technological developments to canalize the general wants they produce. The major economic changes are always intimately associated with cultural shifts. The development of the automobile is often considered the major single economic or cultural event of the twentieth century. Quite possibly electronic communications should be considered second in both categories. (This point of view obviously ignores the social and economic impact of major wars.) Culturally speaking, the automobile was developed early. That is, at a time when it was mechanically satisfactory, it was not yet widely acceptable. The change from horse-drawn to combustion-driven private transportation was too great to be made rapidly. Resistance to early automobiles was great. Restrictive laws and local ordinances demonstrated that the automobile was merely on trial by society as it flashed by at twenty miles an hour on the dirt street. It took fifty years for the nation to make the cultural shifts required by the automobile and to generate the capital for its complete integration, which included billions of dollars in highways and traffic control as well as in productive capacity. Similarly, radio was developed at a culturally early point. Its early use was limited to nonpublic broadcasting because the appropriate elements of society (capital sources, entertainers, advertisers, news suppliers, and potential listeners) were not yet capable of recognizing its potential. Capital requirements were not restrictive in the sense that they were in the development of a full automotive-highway industry. Development obviously could proceed as rapidly as society responded. But it took about twenty-five years to develop a moderately mature broadcasting industry. By comparison, television was introduced at a culturally late date. Social acceptance preceded availability. The development of a mature television industry was slowed not by a reluctant society but by the problems involved in manufacturing television sets, constructing broadcasting stations, developing a supply of cameramen, directors, writers, actors, and the like. In some cities as much as 20 percent of the families owned television sets before they could receive any signal! In Champaign, Illinois, several persons turned in old sets for later models when the local station began broadcasting in 1953. Some of these people had never received a program that was even moderately visible on their old sets.

Others had built antennas to the height of 140 feet in order to receive signals from 125 miles away.

In summary, major capital expenditures in the automotive industry in 1903 would probably have had little effect on economic growth during the subsequent five years. In fact, they might have led to commercial failures. On the other hand, greater capital expenditures in the television industry during 1946–1948 would probably have had good growth returns. The problem of growth is not merely that of increasing the level of investments but also that of developing attractive investment opportunities. This entails the discovery of goods and services for which the culture is ripe.

The consumer is always culture-bound. Probably there will not be enough dried octopus, codpieces, and hookahs sold in Omaha in 1970 to support a single person's activities for a week, yet at one time or another and in one place or another, these have been standard items of consumer use. All of them satisfy normal human wants that are in our culture directed in part toward the purchase of shrimp, hairdressing, neckties, and cigarettes.

The culture always provides approved specific goal objects for any generalized human want. A reasonably cosmopolitan culture provides a host of alternatives serving the same general end, and in an economically mature culture most of the alternatives imply products. For the natural human want for excitement, one can attend a wrestling match, become a sports car enthusiast, take up skiing, purchase a scuba diving outfit, turn on television, or purchase a paperback mystery. One may not engage in a duel, shoot Indians, bait bears, or attend a cockfight. Of course everyone knows most of the specific activities and products approved by his own culture at any particular time.

In addition, the general culture makes relatively stringent demands and encourages certain rather intense general wants. In our culture, success, youthfulness, excitement, and social acceptability are among the most intense general wants cultivated. These wants differ from the usual physiological drives in that they become virtually insatiable. Of course they also vary in intensity with different individuals and even seem to be almost irrelevant to the behavior of a small minority. The difference between such culturally enforced wants and the traditional physiological drives is great. For instance, it is not particularly difficult to determine an adequate diet for almost anyone, given a modicum of information. Almost no one can exist on less than 1200 calories a day or requires more than 4000 (unless the want is a social or psychological one). Further, almost no one is continually interested in food. On the other hand, the vice presidency of a major corporation, paying $145,000 a year, may be far too little success for some; while others refuse a promotion to foreman at a salary of $6,000. Still others will not even take a steady job or attempt to establish any sort of continuous job or relationship. One person may be concerned with success all the waking hours of his day so that he can enjoy no activity that is not somehow related to it. Others may concern themselves with it only some of the time or not at all. The range in intensity and persistence of general cultural goals is enormous. And the mixture of these in individuals can be surprisingly variable. Some individuals pursue youthfulness with the same single-minded devotion with which others pursue excitement or success. Of course, most persons accept the general social goals and pursue them with reasonable intensity and persistence, continually making choices that are acceptable in terms of most of the general cultural values.

The problems of commercial enterprises with regard to cultural requirements would be slight, if modern cultures were as static as primitive cultures, or even as slow-moving as our own culture of the early nineteenth century. The present culture is, however, continually changing — although perhaps principally in its material aspects — at a rate that seems to have been unmatched in history. In part this is the effect of greater familiarity with other cultures, in part it is a response to technological change, in part it stems from increasingly widespread and rapid communication within the culture, and in part it is related to social protest and our greater willingness to accept certain kinds of change. All of these are, of course, facilitated by our relative affluence.

The United States is a nation with a remarkable number of subcultures. Some are imported, some are essentially home-grown. We speak more like one another, in all probability, than did Britons who lived a hundred miles apart in 1400. But our regional subcultures have not been completely eliminated in the steady progress toward cultural homogeneity. The West Coast drinks more gin and vodka, the East more Scotch, and the South more bourbon. Birch beer and cream soda are soft-drink flavors of some importance in New England. They do not exist in Birmingham or Shreveport. Artichokes are such important food items in the Italian section of Manhattan that gang wars occurred over their control in the 1930's. In central Illinois or South Carolina they are rarities that most shoppers stare at in perplexity. Maxwell House coffee has a special blend for its western customers, a darker, stronger roast than is popular in the East. Beef supplied to northern and eastern markets is heavier and hung longer than that available in the South and West, where "baby beef" is popular. College dormitories in the Midwest generally avoid serving lamb, because many of their occupants regard it as inedible. The list of regional taste differences could continue, including almost every type of product sold.

Large-scale movements of people from one section of the country to the other mean that almost any regional custom or preference may spread to other sections — sometimes with considerable rapidity. Blue jeans, brightly colored sports shirts, and the so-called Ivy League cut in men's clothing are examples of regional clothing styles that have become national. Other regional preferences, such as the rural sunbonnet and the Mother Hubbard, have virtually disappeared. Catching these changes and helping them along with the right merchandise at the right time becomes a necessary business function.

Other changes relate to our increasing awareness of other cultures and to a sort of reverse acculturation, in which the nation has accepted enthusiastically some of the customs, clothes, or foods of immigrants who largely give these same things up as they became acculturated. Pizza has become as ubiquitous as the hot dog since World War II. Japanese sandals are on sale in virtually every drug store. African fertility figures have become standard living room bric-a-brac. And shishkabob broils on the outdoor grill.

Many of the cultural shifts arise simply out of changing circumstances, such as the shortening work week and higher income. Casual clothing, boats and outboard motors, power mowers, a host of new home appliances sell more widely largely because of increased income and leisure time. And in the process the nature of day-to-day life takes on new dimensions as new products are more widely adopted. High fidelity and stereo replace the phonograph, and good music becomes a profitable commodity. Foreign cars and sport cars introduce entirely new concepts of the automobile's place in society, changing standards and values as they become accepted. One of the major changes becomes the rate at which society will accept change. New products are searched out rather than resisted. Food stores that in the thirties carried a few hundred different products, now stock thousands. And the former best sellers often disappear. In all probability there never was a culture or a time in which it was so easy to introduce the new, the novel, and the strange in products or services. (This apparent readiness to accept the modern does not, of course, apply to all areas of human activity. The very person who is most eager for the latest in kitchen ranges may violently oppose abstract expressionism in art. The factory that is the home of the most up-to-date machinery may house the most old-fashioned economic or political values.) The entire nature of Americans as consumers seems to have shifted away from reliance on tradition, although this can be true only in a relatively superficial sense.

This does not mean, of course, that every new product will succeed. Most new products still fail. But those that are in step with cultural changes are rapid successes. When a new low-calorie cereal for adults was introduced, it was cleared off the shelf. And a succession of weight control aids seemed just what the customer ordered.

For business the task of anticipating changes and determining consumer wants is difficult, probably more difficult than ever before, since consumers are notoriously unable to indicate what they will want in the future, beyond suggesting that it should be different.

But most new desires are signaled well in advance, if the signals can be interpreted even partly as well as the economic indicators. In general, the direction of cultural change is indicated by various groups or classes that first accept as a distinguishing characteristic what will later become a cultural norm for larger portions of society. It was the moderately well-to-do, the professional and executive groups, who first demonstrated the need for smaller, less expensive cars by purchasing Renaults, Volkswagens, and MGs. It was a little group of Beatniks in San Francisco who made the bongo drum and the recorder and the guitar commercially more important — the first two having been relative curiosities before their adoption as symbols of social revolt or group difference. The ways in which values are passed on from group to group in the process of becoming cultural standards is incompletely understood. At least, it is always easier to use the techniques of the sociologist or anthropologist to explain what has happened than it is to predict what will happen.

In part, this may be related to the meager resources made available for the development of predictive techniques or to the tendency of sociologists and anthropologists to be uninterested in possible commercial applications of their disciplines. Yet if there is a cultural lag between the development of new products and their acceptance, it is probably no greater than the lag between the developing wants of a society and the allocation of resources to satisfy those wants. Both lags have major economic consequences and neither is susceptible to reduction through economic analysis or the operation of the market place. Promotional techniques have been developed to minimize the cultural lag. No known methodology has been applied seriously to the allocative lag, which is considered the province of entrepreneurial opportunity.

Groups and classes carry out the social functions of a culture, enforce or change its standards, alter its values. And in terms of production or marketing, it is normally groups or classes of some sort that serve as the consumer model. Few businesses produce for single individuals, and no economically important one does. Few businesses serve the entire culture with a single product, although those that do are generally large companies. Most business organizations find that they are primarily serving some limited public with more or less common characteristics. The markets for Thunderbirds, Chanel No. 5, Serutan, Old Grandad, Hart, Schafner and Marx, and Frosted Flakes tend to be limited markets that can be described best by combinations of social and economic terms.

Class

There is a general notion that most new ideas, values, and products are first accepted by the highest classes in a society and slowly filter down to the lowest as persons in each class emulate those above them. The notion is oversimplified, of course, but there are reasonable approximations of this kind of social leadership in consumption. Mechanical refrigerators were quite widely accepted in well-to-do suburbs ten years before they became standard household equipment. During the first few years of its development, television was a class medium; the average income of families with television sets was far above that of families without them. The small foreign car was first accepted, and still largely is, by the upper-middle class, rather than by the lower classes where its price would seem to make it more appropriate. Wall-to-wall carpeting was once the exclusive purchase of the wealthy and the near wealthy, as was high fidelity.

The probable reason for this tendency for new items to be used first by the upper classes lies in the fact that until quite recently only they had the money to spend on luxuries. It is quite obvious that nothing new can be other than a luxury in social terms. An automatic washing machine was once a luxury rather than the "necessity" that it now is. The fact that it was accepted first by the middle-class housewife is related to several social and economic trends. At the time when washing machines were first being introduced, domestic help was still plentiful, and most upper- and upper-middle-class families had at least part-time help. Many lower-middle-class families had a washing woman or a cleaning woman or both. The old-fashioned washer with a wringer attached may well have been accepted first by the upper classes, although there is not adequate information on the subject. But the automatic washer was introduced at a time when domestic servants were rapidly disappearing — becoming one of the true luxuries. In comparison, the automatic washing machine was only a semi-luxury. The result seems to have been that the wealthy let their domestic servants continue to use the washer-wringer, while those with considerably less income — often even the lower-middle class — turned earliest to the automatic machine. In an affluent society, the new product can enter at any social level above the poorest, and may not even be highly appropriate to the upper levels. Instant mashed potatoes and TV dinners are undoubtedly luxuries whose ingredients could be purchased for much less. But it is doubtful that the wealthy — with the greater luxury of a full-time cook or chef in the kitchen — ever resort to such time-saving and unappetizing expedients. In fact, many of the upper-middle class, which has high standards for food, still refuse to purchase the manifestly indifferent prepared foods that have become so popular.

In general, the different classes have different tastes and often do not aspire to the tastes of classes above their own. Most Americans are poorly informed about the taste of either higher or lower classes and have a strong tendency to deride that of any but their own class, subculture, and group. It is a serious mistake to believe that all persons are interested in moving up some social ladder. Far more undoubtedly are quite satisfied with their own place in society and are afraid of losing it by movement in either direction. Most lower-middle-class families would undoubtedly refuse to hang an original Kandinsky or Modigliani on their walls if it were given to them.

Probably they would not like the painting, but stronger yet would be their fear of the reaction of lower-middle-class friends.

Rainwater indicates some of the differences between the wives of blue-collar and white-collar men.[4] It is obvious from his description that the mode of life of the lower-middle and upper-middle class has marked differences. Taste in furniture and home furnishings varies greatly between the two, probably because they seldom visit each other's homes and because the communications media that best describe upper-middle-class standards in this regard, such as *American Home, House and Garden,* and *House Beautiful,* are relatively unknown to the lower-middle class. Thus, the lower-middle-class housewife tends to prettify her home with exactly the items an upper-middle-class housewife would be least likely to buy — the kinds of things, in fact, that would make her shudder. Clearly the upper-middle-class housewife is the market for Danish modern, the Eames chair and foreign stainless steel flatware (if she does not limit herself to sterling). The lower-middle-class housewife tends toward the formica-covered dinette set, silver-plate in a relatively fancy design, and highly conventional furniture.

To a great extent, families tend to preserve their class tastes whether their income rises or falls. The young upper-middle-class couple on a restricted budget generally does not buy the same furniture, food, or clothing that a lower-middle-class family with the same income would buy. On the other hand, the lower-middle-class family with increased income is unlikely to adjust its tastes or move to an upper-middle-class neighborhood. Bruce Weale reports that a fairly standard reaction to increased income is the customer's feeling that products that he can now afford are still "too good" for him.[5] In other cases, what the person with rising income conceives as appropriate luxuries are merely more expensive versions of what he would have purchased previously.

Clearly, class serves as a sort of screen (in much the same sense that culture does) that limits the choice of the individual. Unlike culture, however, which does not imply great emotional context, since the things that it excludes are generally unknown or unthought of,

[4]Lee Rainwater, Richard P. Coleman, and Gerald Handel, *Workingman's Wife,* New York, Oceana, 1959.

[5]W. Bruce Weale, "Are We Good Enough for Your Product," *Salesmanship: Modern Viewpoints on Personal Communication* (Steven J. Shaw and Joseph W. Thompson, Eds.) New York, Holt, 1960.

class distinctions are of tremendous importance to individuals of all classes. Almost no one has learned the lessons of his class perfectly or can keep up with its changing values. Since loss of social position may attend serious evaluative mistakes and, since even small losses in status or prestige are regarded as serious, class limits on choices become persistent and intense factors in the hierarchy of personal wants. Concern with the outer manifestations of class — neighborhood, clothing, and furniture — is great, even among those who seem to make the right choices without apparent effort or interest. Perhaps the concern is greatest for the upper-middle class because its members normally have less economic security than either the class immediately above or below it (death of the male head of the family is less likely to influence the income or class standing of the lower-middle- or upper-class family), because it has available to it a broad range of choices where error is possible and because it probably experiences a more rapidly changing set of material values.

The upper-middle class is probably less conservative than most of the other classes, so that any given value is less likely to persist than in the upper-upper or lower-middle class. It is undoubtedly the most mobile of the classes, being less tied to family interests and family businesses than the upper class and more aware of distant opportunities than the lower-middle and the lower classes. Its general wants are probably more intense and its specific wants more variable than those of other classes. The most fashionably dressed women in the nation (except those for whom fashion is a professional requirement) are probably members of the upper-middle class who have considerable or great wealth. This may explain why Dallas is known as a high-fashion city.

Perhaps nothing is as distracting commercially as the speed with which the upper-middle class can change its allegiances and interests. Floral, sculptured carpeting may be quite acceptable one year and out of the question the next. It is likely that the styles and items most rapidly rejected after adoption are those that grow in popularity in the lower-middle class. The lower-upper class has the same tendency to avoid anything that becomes too popular in the upper-middle class. In determining the wants of these groups, almost the only safe generality (and it is a shaky one) is that the most highly approved products next year will not be the most highly approved this year by any of the sublevels of these two classes. This does not mean, of course, that a particular item will not still be purchased by members of a subclass that purchased it last year — especially if the item is not a fashion item. It does mean, however, that the item will no longer possess the social magic that it did a year earlier. An Atlanta department store executive drove a Triumph with real pleasure when it was the only Triumph registered in the State of Georgia. When the popularity of the make grew more rapidly than he had expected, he was forced to turn it in for a less common sports car.

At present there are no satisfactory ways to predict the rate at which the popularity of an item will move from one class to another. For this reason, fashion merchandise (and an increasingly large percentage of merchandise has a fashion aspect) experiences sales variations that are difficult to predict. The same tailfins that boosted Chrysler Corporation sales one year apparently hurt them the next. In fact, the automobile may have seen the end of its dominant role as a social symbol. Large numbers of upper-middle-class families obviously consider it of secondary importance already. Clearly, a failure of the automotive manufacturers to anticipate any changing role of their product could have considerable economic impact. Perhaps one of the key predictors of the industry's sales lies not in over-all automotive sales but in a closer look at what particular kinds of people are doing with regard to automobile purchases. Current behavior of the lower-middle-class might suggest what the upper middle is going to stop doing. Or perhaps examination of the behavior of particular consumers would be more indicative, since changes normally move through the social network in much the same way; that is, from individual to individual within the immediate context of some group.

Group

Several demographic divisions that do not relate to culture or class are often erroneously referred to as groups. They are not groups in the social sense that they interact, but only in the sense that they are made up of persons or families that have certain similarities. Such "groups" can be tremendously important in the role of consumers. For instance, in the middle fifties, rug and carpet sales declined, apparently to the surprise of the industry. It was well known that the years of heaviest buying of the product came shortly after marriage, but no one in the industry had paid sufficient attention to the fact that new family formations were falling off during the fifties, simply because there were decreasing numbers of people of marriageable age. The number of marriages would begin to increase again as the World War II babies began to reach 18, 19, and 20.

Single young people, young married couples, families with young children, those with teen-age children, and those whose children have left home, and finally the retired family all spend their income in different ways. In recent years, businesses have become increasingly aware of the product preferences of various age groups and families at various stages in the life cycle. In a mature economy and a reasonably affluent one, such groups undoubtedly deserve considerable attention. They are not, however, the kind of groups that influence consumer behavior, except where individuals of the same age or similar family situation are members of a real social group.

Katz and Lazarsfeld report the ways in which intimate, face-to-face groups develop their purchasing criteria for some kinds of products.[6] The indications are that social leadership may be a more complex phenomenon than it is sometimes thought to be. For instance, most information and advice seem to move within class lines rather than across them. Advice is not sought from social superiors but from social equals. And the specific advisor seems to vary with the subject on which advice is being sought. A woman is likely to receive fashion or cosmetic information from younger intimates, such as daughters, nieces, or younger close acquaintances. Advice or information about cooking or food is more likely to be passed from the elder to the younger.

Of course, advice and information are not the only ways in which social influence operates. The mere serving of beef Stroganoff at a supper may be enough to cause guests to try it in their own homes. The mere presence of a braided cotton rug on the floor of a particular home is enough to change its value in the eyes of friends or acquaintances. The fact that a respected doctor has a seven-year-old car in his drive may tend to change the significance of the Cadillac next door.

But material possessions are commonly matters for discussion. One person asks another where he bought a suit, how he likes a car, whether a swimming pool is a lot of trouble, what the rates are on his fire insurance, or what ingredients went into a particular pie crust. A surgeon reports that in his hospital cafeteria the conversation largely concerns investments and especially the stock market when members

[6]Elihu Katz and Paul F. Lazarsfeld, *Personal Influence*, New York, Free Press, 1955.

of the staff meet. It is not surprising that decisions to buy or sell and
what to buy or sell should be made as much on the statements of intimate friends or business acquaintances as on the advice of brokers or
investment counselors. A study by Hugh Sargent shows that subscribers to *Consumer Reports* are somewhat more likely than others to
purchase appliances and other items recommended by that publica-
tion.[7] The difference is so slight, however, that one is forced to wonder
what kinds of information, what kinds of influence, counteracted the
Consumer Reports rating if so many subscribers failed to follow the
advice they had paid for. At least one element in the situation was
probably the conflicting experiences of close friends and acquaintances.

All consumer industries are aware of sleepers, products that without extensive promotion generate a considerable following as the word
is passed from friend to friend with the growing effect of the chain
letter. Especially does this seem to occur in the theater, motion
picture, and book industries. *South Pacific* was generally panned by
critics who attended its opening performance on Broadway.

Less intimate social organizations, such as professional groups,
may strongly influence the course of a product's life. Doctors were
the greatest factor in changing banana flakes from a regular to a
pediatric product. College professors pass the word from one to another and a textbook becomes popular or lags. Electrical engineers
develop a strong preference for one type of switch or circuit breaker.
Of course, it is common for commercial interests to approach such
groups in much the same way that they reach consumers: by advertising. But the way in which the first persons who try the product react
and whether they recommend it to friends is often the real test of
success.

All groups have their experimenters who try out the new and
evaluate it for others. But these key individuals are difficult to locate
and their relative influence is hard to determine, since even the least
influential may be early purchasers. Early sales of pink shirts to
men apparently indicated that the fashion leaders had accepted the
proposed style. Whether this was true and these persons simply
failed to influence their more conservative followers or whether the
early buyers were largely those who lacked fashion influence is not
clear. In a society like ours, many persons are not solidly integrated

[7]Hugh W. Sargent, *Consumer-Product Rating Publications and Buying Behavior*, Urbana, Ill., Bureau of Business and Economic Research, University of
Illinois, 1959.

into social groups of any particular strength. They may draw their values, often mistakenly, from some reference group to which they do not actually belong. Such persons may infer from magazine advertisements or other impersonal sources what their reference group is doing. And rather than accepting the evaluation of mere acquaintances, they may seek out the original source of information for approval. Needless to say, they usually get it. Thus, a relative isolate may purchase an item believing that it is a suitable one, and, since he is an isolate, fail to get appropriate feedback from the reference group, which is unaware of his existence. In an urban society characterized by moderate social mobility, there are many such isolates whose purchasing behavior may have little to do with general social acceptance by any group, class, subclass, or subculture. The same number of sales to social leaders would indicate acceptance of an entirely different order.

The relative disorganization of our society makes it a particularly difficult one for business to supply with precision, since sales alone are not so important as information on what part of the social body is purchasing. In the end it is the group — and most persons belong to a number of groups — that accepts or rejects, approves or disapproves. Group values are not always clear from the behavior of particular members of the group, since each member has a somewhat different role. The group tolerates certain kinds of deviant behavior on the part of any member, and the new norms will appear first as deviant behavior. But not all of this deviant behavior will be accepted. One person who dresses somewhat differently than other members may never set the fashion. His sartorial difference is merely tolerated. A new fashion adopted by another, may signal the fact that the entire group (or most of it) will follow.

Group control of individual wants is more specific and stronger in smaller and more intimate organizations. Particular families never eat sardines, never wear high-fashion clothing, or always buy Gulf gasoline and Palmolive soap. In a college, the members of a single fraternity or sorority dress more alike than the entire student body does. It is no accident that the juvenile gang wears what amounts to a uniform. Anyone working in New York is normally surprised at the frequency with which he runs into friends on the street or in restaurants, not realizing that all his close acquaintances inhabit only the smallest portion of the metropolis, patronizing the same stores and restaurants, purchasing much the same products, in short, pursuing the same relatively specific goals and subgoals that their group membership makes desirable.

In summary, economic value is a function of cultural, class, and group values. Consumer choices, therefore, always have a large social content that constantly alters economic realities and typically makes the discovery of consumer demand difficult.

5 ▶

Work

A mature economy needs labor of many sorts, in many different locations, for varying periods of time. In general, about the only systematic method for getting people to select one job rather than another, to move from one place to another, is to offer money or its equivalent in fringe benefits of some sort. Yet it is commonly recognized that economic considerations have only limited effect on the occupation the individual chooses, the company he works for, or the amount of time and energy he is willing to expend on the job.

Career Choice

It is literally impossible for a young person to have a reasonable knowledge of the more than 50,000 job classifications listed in the *Dictionary of Occupational Titles*. In truth he is likely to have only the crudest notions of what more than a few occupations demand or what rewards they provide. Further, the young person may know considerably less about normal career sequences than he does about specific occupations or jobs. The route to becoming a building contractor, advertising man, banker, or industrial salesman may be completely unknown even though the occupation itself is adequately comprehended. It is largely for this reason that an elderly Georgia farmer reports that he was forty before he realized that there was any way other than raising cotton to make a living. He grew up knowing the other occupations within his relatively narrow world without seeing the career path by which he could reach them. While such limited horizons are probably less common today than they were fifty years ago, many children of migratory farm workers, unskilled

50

laborers, and certain ethnic groups must operate under restrictions that are comparable.

At first, the child is aware only of those jobs held by members of the immediate family and a few publicly observable occupations such as those of the policeman or the retail sales clerk. In most cases, since imitation of parental roles is normal development, the child simply assumes that fathers go to work on the train every morning and work in a big office building, or take care of sick people, or milk cows. And most are well along in the role of the parent or their sex by the time they realize that there is some choice in the matter. Even after learning that a choice is possible, the child is normally subject to a number of years of coaching by parents and others before he has even passing interest in his future occupation. Children seldom ask other children what they are going to be when they grow up. It is the adults who ask the question and then indicate by their response whether the goal is appropriate. Some families exert pressure, either open or subtle, to ensure the child's choosing the same occupation as the father — or choosing a different one. All families make clear their occupational standards. The accountant's son is not permitted to aspire to be a carpenter. And he recognizes that he does not want to be a carpenter, probably thinking of his preference as personal if he thinks of its source at all. The family carefully nurtures the class distinctions, emphasizing the importance of the right kind of job.

While much of this directive activity is intentional, since parents are normally concerned in high degree with the child's future, much is merely incidental to a way of life. The doctor's son who hears his father called out at all hours and sees that he misses meals and engagements may have accepted this onerous aspect of medicine as normal to everyday living before he has ever thought seriously of his own career. The way the father dresses when he leaves for work, the hours or days that he is gone, are minimal intrusions of work into family life that prepare the child for a similar future. And everyday comments about friends of the family and others make it clear that their occupation and their status are intimately bound together — to the young it must often seem that they are identical.

The right kind of job is certainly one that has at least approximately the same class as that of the father; but, surprising to some people, it is not likely to belong to a much higher class. Parents are not typically overambitious for their children. The lower-class family that pushes its children to become doctors or lawyers is the exception.

After all, few families know how to advocate effectively those occupations they only vaguely comprehend, since the strongest job advocacy is intimately bound up in the values and personality characteristics the family fosters. The parents who place great value on money and encourage a child to become a doctor "because doctors make a lot of money" are probably helping the child develop a value that will militate against his entering the medical profession — not because doctors universally lack interest in money, but because the onerous process of becoming one is not easily sustained by financial goals alone.

The restrictions generally placed on the individual's occupational goals by early family life are of three sorts. These relate to the values of the family and its familiarity with job types, the family's class or social status, and its cultural and subcultural background. The banker's son will seldom be free to seriously consider life as a professional musician or theatrical director, the middle-class youth will find it relatively hard to imagine himself in either a lower-class or an upper-class occupation, the young Jew seldom thinks of farming even on the affluent scale possible with training and capital, and the rancher's son is unlikely to go into retailing.

Social organization being what it is, the friends and acquaintances of the young person are generally capable of broadening his occupational considerations only slightly, since neighborhoods and school districts are populated by pretty much the same subcultural and class groups. Therefore, many of the general restrictions placed on the individual's concept of appropriate jobs by the family will be heavily reinforced by friends.

The school, especially the high school or college, is often the first place where any reasonably broad understanding of unfamiliar jobs is acquired. But even the broadened occupational horizon developed in such institutions should not be thought of as at all inclusive. It is quite possible for a college student to major in management without developing any adequate notion of what various bank executives do. A graduating electrical engineer may have a good notion of only some of his occupational possibilities. Quite often the graduate of a liberal arts college has little more career information than he had when he entered four years earlier. Nor does vocational guidance do more than ameliorate the situation. One of the occupational interest tests commonly given to college students lists advertising as appropriate for certain relatively specific types of people without recognizing that even so limited a field as advertising contains at least half-a-dozen highly distinct types of work not particularly appropriate for the same kinds of persons.

Most people end their college or high-school careers without knowing what a medical artist, product manager, trust officer, underwriter, foreign service officer, or production expediter is or does. Yet all these jobs and hundreds of others as unfamiliar must ultimately be filled largely by persons who end their formal education without knowing of the existence of their own future occupation.

Under such circumstances it is manifestly impossible for the new worker to choose the career that will be economically to his best advantage. He has been steered strongly and has little information about future possibilities or even present pay in more than a few jobs. If he is a high-school graduate or has less formal education, he looks for work in his own city or a nearby one in a way that indicates that the occupation (in the form of available openings) chooses the individual as much as the reverse. Increasingly, if he is a college graduate, he is interviewed by a company that visits the campus and solicits him — often having to explain the job for which he is being considered because he has only vague notions about what it entails. Again, he is not so much the chooser as the chosen, with only the roughest idea of whether he has made a wise economic choice.

On the other hand, he is generally quite aware of the kind of social choice that he has made. As an hourly laborer in an air-frame plant, he knows that he stands above parking lot attendants and below bank tellers; as a management trainee for a large corporation, he knows that he stands on about a par with professional men. One large corporation has some difficulty in getting college graduates as executive trainees because it starts them out for a rather lengthy period driving a truck. The pay is good, but the temporary social status is not satisfactory.

An amazingly large number of careers are not really planned at all — nor do they simply happen. They are the result of normal group action. The first-time worker takes a job in the same organization for which his father, or older brother or uncle, works or for which some friend works — the exact nature of the job being of less importance than the social relationship that brings it to attention. And, often, the situation works out quite well. Some organizations look upon their present employees as the best source of future employees, feeling that the people who come to them through such social connections normally turn out to be more permanent, better workers with fewer absences. The unknown individual who comes in response to a news-paper advertisement is less likely to commit himself wholeheartedly to the work situation. Probably more than 75 percent of first-time workers get jobs through relatives, friends, or chance encounters.[1]

In other words, quite frequently the only occupational or general career decision made by the individual is to accept or reject a partic-ular job and to follow where it leads. It seems to lead only in the direction of other jobs that entail approximately the social standing his family has. While no one can deny that the American dream of rags to riches is constantly being fulfilled for a small percentage of the population, students of vertical mobility agree with Davidson and Anderson that: "There is also apparent a fairly close agreement, in general, between family circumstances and occupational status of fathers and the ultimate occupational attainments of sons."[2]

The process of getting a job — or, from the company standpoint, the process of hiring an employee — differs greatly according to the na-ture of the job (its permanence, importance, and so forth), the kind of institution doing the hiring, and a number of other factors. The situa-tion in which protocol is at a minimum is that in which the job has little social or economic significance, will last only a relatively brief period of time, and can be performed by almost anyone. Agricultural labor used in the picking of crops and other routine tasks is often hired on sight. It makes little difference how many persons are hired (within reasonably broad limits) and the worker and the hiring organization accept minimal responsibility to each other. Jobs of this sort are normally sought only by the lower class or students out of school. (There is a relatively high social value placed in this nation on having done some kind of manual labor during youth. Even upper-class families may encourage or force sons to take lower-class jobs during their late teens or early twenties. The same value does not apply to girls, who are generally discouraged from taking such jobs at any time.)

[1]Joseph Shister, *Economics of the Labor Market*, Philadelphia, Lippincott, 1956, p. 18.

[2]Percy E. Davidson and H. Dewey Anderson, *Occupational Mobility in an American Community*, Stanford, California, Stanford University Press, 1937, p. 103. Other principal sources include W. Lloyd Warner and James C. Abegglen, *Occupational Mobility in American Business and Industry*, Minneapolis, University of Minnesota Press, 1955; Natalie Rogoff, *Recent Trends in Occupational Mobility*, New York, Free Press, 1953.

Jobs that are of indefinite duration are generally filled through more exacting processes that include extensive written applications, interviews, and often a testing program. Some even require remarkably fanciful first contacts. In fact, in certain situations it is improper for the job hunter to admit that he is looking or the prospective organization to mention that it has a vacancy. And the list of requisites may be astonishing, including such commonplace social requirements as race or religion and continuing to one's views on socialized medicine or one's abstention from tobacco or alcohol. (For years no one who worked for Henry Ford or Harvey Firestone was allowed to smoke on the job — or expected to smoke off the job for that matter. New associate professors at Wake Forest were required to take an oath stating that they believed in the Baptist interpretation of the Bible and that they neither smoked nor drank.)

At the lowest level, jobs may be open to virtually anyone who applies simply because the low salary means that applicants will normally be undifferentiated in their lack of skill and low social status. But even here it is likely that a well-dressed person who spoke articulately and reasonably knowledgeably would be turned down simply because he so obviously did not fit the job's social requirements.

The manager of the laundry or motel or restaurant looking for an ironer or room maid or waitress will normally put great store in the recommendations of one of his present workers. And the prospective employee will be particularly interested in the report his friend makes about the nature of the job. But the hiring protocol may be brief and simple, requiring only a cursory interview in which the two participants size one another up. Almost everyone is at least theoretically familiar with the shape-up or hiring hall in which social relationships become all important and the outsider has difficulty in gaining approval. Under closed shop conditions, the plasterer's union in San Francisco for a number of years limited new union memberships to immediate relatives of existing members. Such social exclusiveness is not dissimilar to that of the country club or the social fraternity although it may be designed to deliver different rewards.

The principal purpose of the job interview seems to be the determination of social appropriateness when close personal relations do not already exist. There is no intention here of suggesting that social appropriateness is not important to most jobs or that a critical examination of the prospective employee is a waste of time. Far from it; the work group is always a social group, and the employee who doesn't "get along" is a more frequent cause of trouble than the employee who cannot handle the technical aspects of his job. In all probability the same factor affects the employee's satisfaction with his job. The job interview, then, is probably the single most important aspect of the hiring or job-getting process simply because it bears a close relationship to the social character of the work.

The interview is, nonetheless, an interesting socio-economic phenomenon. Both parties enter the situation well briefed, armed with specific questions and specific answers that they anticipate utilizing. And both are dressed for the occasion. A college student being interviewed on the campus does not dress as usual for classes but carefully dons a conservative business suit, white shirt, unspectacular tie, and well-shined shoes. (At all levels of work overdressing for the interview is common practice.) This may be inappropriate for the job he will get, but it is at least like the dress of the interviewer (generally on the young side in order to establish rapport with the student) and essentially what he may wear after one or two promotions. Both interviewer and interviewee play carefully selected roles. Sincerity is the key characteristic of both roles, and humor is acceptable only if it is highly conventional. As in most meetings in business between people who do not know one another, the time is broken up into a purely social prologue followed by a discussion of the matter of the meeting. Since the length of the prologue is directly related to the importance of the position to be filled, in the campus interview it may be no more than a few introductory words.

The interviewer normally starts by describing the corporation he represents, its general operations, and the particular job for which he is interviewing. After giving the student a chance to ask questions on these matters, he then asks a series of questions about the student's interests, abilities, and goals. Where the two have a common interest or a common acquaintance the subject is dwelt on at some length, just as it is when anyone meets a new acquaintance. There is, of course, a large number of factual details of interest to both parties and of consequence to the outcome of the interview. Salary, specific nature of the job, likelihood of promotion, amount of traveling required, location and probable future locations, fringe benefits, and the like are usually discussed. Beyond these, and at least as important, is the attempt of both parties to determine what it would be like to work with the other. The student's unasked question is basically: "Will I enjoy working with you people?" And the interviewer's is the reverse: "I wonder how he'll get along with us?"

It should be pointed out that "getting along" in modern corporate life is based on nothing so superficial as being a good drinking partner or a great addition to the party. "Getting along" refers to the individual's ability to take directions easily, work with reasonable diligence, and conform to work-group standards without undue chafing.

After the first screening interview, the student will probably visit the corporations he is still interested in — and which have a continuing interest in him. While the original interview may take only half-an-hour, the subsequent interview may take all day and in its own particular way test the possible social relationship. Of course, both parties explore what are normally considered the practical aspects of the situation, but in talking with either the interviewer or the student later, one often finds that what sticks in their mind is:

"He has a good appearance, looks you right in the eye when he talks with you."

"Maybe a little rough around the edges, but smart enough to smooth out in a hurry."

"The vice-president was a regular guy. Took my questions seriously and answered them as though he were really interested in me."

"They have a swell bunch of guys in the office. You know, the kind of people you can get along with."

If the social objectives and social protocols of hiring potential executives are of moderate interest, the characteristics of the process when a present executive position or other important job is under consideration can sometimes seem a real phantasy in its indirection. One of the most interesting characteristics of many such protocols is the pretense that the interview is not a job interview. Typically, at the higher levels of business (or government or education) the prospective employee must not admit that he is in the market for a job, nor does the potential employer suggest that there is an opening. The original contact is normally made in some such fashion as this. The person who wants to change jobs mentions to a few close friends in the industry that he would not be averse to a change — that he has an open mind and might consider an offer of the right kind. If the friend he mentions this to is a true intimate, he may confess the extent of his unease or disappointment with his present job and explain the full circumstances that make him want to move. The friends will mention the situation to their friends, and the rumor will spread that so-and-so is looking around. A company with the right kind of opening will then make its approach. (It is usually wrong for the applicant to approach the company directly, even if he knows of an opening for which he would be suited.) Often the approach will be made by a mutual friend rather than the company that will do the hiring, in order to discover whether the prospect is willing to consider the particular job. And early direct meetings between the prospect and the company may be on some subject other than the job itself, such as a conference talk or advice on a project. Members of management consulting firms are often hired away by the companies that consult them, largely because they become well acquainted with the company's officers and demonstrate that they can work harmoniously with "other members of the team." C. Wright Mills was convinced that the tendency to select people one knows for jobs of great trust has created a power elite that moves smoothly from one position to another in the upper reaches of government, business, and military structures.[3] The entree to this group was, in his view, essentially social, might depend in fact on such things as the kind of bridge game one played. Caplow and McGee describe the ritualistic ways in which major universities go about hiring faculty members, the nature of the interviewing process and evaluation.[4] Quite obviously social standing within the discipline is of enormous importance in the evaluation of professors. And the interviewing techniques are so indirect that an individual may be considered for a particular job, interviewed through one pretense or another, and rejected without ever knowing whether he was being considered or what position he was being considered for. The situation that makes such indirect interviewing possible is that the prospect's technical capacities are not in question so much as his ability to fit in. Such precautions may seem absurd to anyone who takes the purely utilitarian point of view and has not seen the distraught organization whose social fabric has been torn by the introduction of a competent new officer into a group of other competent people without reasonably full acceptance. Small differences of opinion of the variety tolerated within most close groups can become matters of violent protest and time-consuming effort — even of group dissolution — when the social adhesives of friendship and mutual loyalty are missing.

[3]C. Wright Mills, *Power Elite*, New York, Oxford University Press, 1956, especially Chapters 6–10.

[4]Theodore Caplow and Reece J. McGee, *Academic Market Place*, New York, Basic, 1958.

Rewards for Work

Not only are career choices and specific job decisions carried out in a social context and under the influence of social goals, but the entire work situation is actually a social one of some complexity for which there are no interchangeable parts. Perhaps more accurately, the work situation always exists within two distinct social frameworks: the formal organization of the institution itself and the informal organization that automatically springs up wherever people exist together.[5]

Most of what is returned to the worker for his efforts comes through either the formal or informal organization. The formal organization pays the worker and in addition gives promotions, awards for superior performance or length of service, work assignments to which status attaches, and some variety of fringe benefits and privileges. It might be argued that the firm provides much of the recognition the worker receives outside the work situation through the quality of its products or services and its public relations and advertising programs. Praise from superiors may be considered a function of either the informal or the formal organization, depending upon circumstances. Certainly it is more personal than any other return granted by the formal organization, and it may be given in the face of punishment by the formal organization. On the other hand, the formal organization may well make special efforts to train its supervisors and executives in the judicious use of praise.

Rewards from the informal organization are normally less specific than those given by the formal organization. They amount first to more than routine recognition by the work group. Special friendships, sympathy and support in the case of difficulties on or off the job, and recognition for work abilities or other characteristics unnoticed by management may all stem from the informal group.

None of this should be taken to indicate that the pay check has anything less than prime importance among the rewards for work.

[5]There is no clear dividing line between formal and informal organization or formal and informal groups or behavior. For this reason some authors, such as Dubin (Robert Dubin, *The World of Work*, Englewood Cliffs, N. J., Prentice-Hall, 1958), prefer to elaborate categories including nonformal behavior as a step between formal and informal, although they do not go to the extent of suggesting the existence of nonformal groups. Whyte (William Foote Whyte, *Men at Work*, Homewood, Ill., Dorsey, 1961), on the other hand, dispenses with the terms "formal" and "informal" altogether. While there are sound reasons for either the Whyte or Dubin terminology, neither seems preferable to the dichotomy used here for all purposes of analysis.

But the persons who are not in some degree responsive to these rewards or to the many corollary punishments that derive from either the formal or informal organization are unusual.

When the youngster from Westfield, Massachusetts, decides to work in the tobacco fields for a summer, he finds himself thrown in with a diversity of workers that includes others like himself, a number of local hands of both sexes, Puerto Ricans from New York, young girls from Pennsylvania who are brought in by bus and housed in fairly attractive camps, and a number of other groups of various sizes and descriptions. The number and heterogeneity of people involved would create a completely unstable situation were they not organized into smaller groups of fifteen or twenty. The typical group will be "Pennsy" girls or Puerto Ricans or local boys or local girls. Each group has a straw boss and several groups together have a foreman. Each group contains either as a part of or in addition to its principal members a few old hands. These latter are of major supervisory importance, although carried on no table of organization. Their job, much like that of the military cadre, is to help develop the informal social organization of the crew in such a way that its principal goals and objectives are in phase with the economic goals of the tobacco company. Conversation is generally tolerated and new workers quickly make friends and work along with them. Kidding of a rough but good-natured sort is the form of the day, but is carefully carried out without jeopardizing the job. Every worker learns rapidly the extreme value of every leaf of shade-grown tobacco. Stepping on a plant or carelessly tearing a leaf become errors that appall not only the bosses but also fellow workers. And typical, informal-group pride in the crop, its value and importance, tempers the activities of the most boisterous teen-ager. The teamwork involved in the sheds, where the leaves flow from the fields to sewers, who sew them on laths, to the hanging crews that pass them up to the hanger, requires that everyone cooperate to keep in step with other activities. A hanging crew will go for a drink of water only when there is a natural work interruption, more out of a sense of group loyalty than fear for their job. It is a peculiar tradition of the group that everyone must express great hatred for the job and tobacco ("tobacco" normally refers to the entire process of planting, stringing, picking, sewing, and hanging, as well as to the crop itself). But everyone senses the real joy of working together, joking and talking, telling outrageous tales that others profess to believe. A single remark can make the whole shed roar in the way that only a reasonably intimate group can achieve. Within days after the first of the season, everyone is known by his first name, including all those in supervisory position. Clearly, the factor that brings some workers back year after year is the easy camaraderie of the fields and the barns, rather than the relatively low wages — although these obviously are important also.

All jobs have a number of things in common with work in the tobacco fields. Every job has some location in a formal organization, and all of the people who hold jobs have some position in the informal social organization that spontaneously arises. Each worker gains, in addition to his pay, whatever satisfactions or dissatisfactions accrue to his positions in the formal and informal structures. In all probability it will be these positions and satisfactions that will hold him to the job or encourage him to look elsewhere, lead to his reluctant or wholehearted cooperation, and vitally influence the course of his life outside the work situation.

Similarly, social pressures of various sorts will invariably influence the individual in his continuation or change of jobs in such a way that the paycheck he receives can be thought of as but one of the variables influencing work decisions.

The nature of the situation within the firm can be particularly difficult to assess simply because increased status within either the formal or informal organization is liable to implicate higher salary.

The satisfied worker at almost any level can be regarded as one who gains certain real satisfactions through the organization he works for. First of these, of course, is his salary or wages. Second are the satisfactions he receives on the job itself. One may want to consider Veblen's instinct for craftsmanship as the source of some of these rewards, but it would seem to make better sense to regard even this as largely social — simply because there are relatively few people who are capable of feeling completely satisfied with a particular piece of work unless someone reacts favorably. (Favorable reactions are not limited to the unimaginative and sterile flattery that is often identified with human relations. Crude and abusive vulgarity may become honorific currency even in the executive suite.) On-the-job satisfactions are undoubtedly several: membership in a cohesive group, recognition for specific tasks accomplished and for general level of ability, belief that what one is doing is important.

Most work groups learn to work together in a relatively rewarding way. The contacts are generally enjoyable. And if the byplay is often less rowdy than that of the tobacco fields, it is sometimes more so. But even the fact that people know one's name, are reasonably cooperative, fulfill his expectations, and generally know what to expect of him makes for an inherently satisfactory situation. Especially in an increasingly anonymous world, the mere fact that one is known and responded to in much the same way day after day can provide considerable reassurance, since anomie, which results from a lack of social attachment, is obviously one of the great demoralizing states of modern society. In fact, anticipated negative responses are obviously preferred to no response at all. Even the consistent surliness of a department manager or immediate superior can become acceptable recognition, reinforcing the values and norms of the work place. The social pleasures of being envied, respected, or liked can sometimes be dispensed with. But the security that comes from being noticed and responded to in expected ways is an absolute social necessity.

Job Satisfaction and Work Behavior

Having taken a job, and having become imbedded in a complex system of social and economic rewards and punishments, the worker is usually incapable of responding to all the influences discussed here or constantly to even a limited number of them. Much of his behavior will be strongly influenced by his own expectations, his socially derived goals, and the immediate pressures placed upon him. While these may occasionally point in the same direction, it is probably more common that they pull and tug against one another or that they are equivocal or vague in the behaviors they suggest. A few examples may show the nature of the difficulty.

Incentive pay at piece-work rates is frequently used to maximize worker productivity. A worker is guaranteed his normal hourly pay as a minimum but can earn more by greater productivity. The effect of such an incentive system cannot be determined in advance for many reasons. The folk wisdom of the work-group may suggest, accurately or inaccurately, that productivity much beyond the point at which incentive payments start will lead either to a lowering of the piece rate or to an earlier layoff. Further, the informal group usually has its own ideas about how fast a person should work, and this becomes a social standard. There is substantial evidence that workers subconsciously adjust their rates in the direction of those of workers near them. A worker will work faster than his own norm when placed next to a rapid worker and slower than his own norm when placed next to a slower worker. In addition, there are strong indications that the social integration of the worker in the informal group, his religious background, social class, and political preference are related to his working pace under an incentive system.[6]

Group norms may become taboos that prevent most workers from increasing their output. Those who consistently defy the group in this regard are generally social isolates on the job and are known as rate-busters. But under some circumstances someone who is closely associated with the informal group may be permitted to maximize his economic return for a short time, especially if he is well thought of and has what the group regards as a special financial problem. One of the difficulties with incentive systems is that high productivity usually is not seen by the group as importantly affecting its long-term economic situation. And even the well-motivated individual may fail to respond strongly, since rate-busting is neither the route to promotion nor to pay increases and incurs the displeasure of the informal organization.

On the other hand, piece-work rates may become so attractive that workers will as a group respond with unexpectedly high production that sends paychecks soaring. Since piece-work rates are set by the organization, unanticipated productivity should be particularly welcome to management. This would seem to be the case although the labor costs per unit remain constant or increase, since the fixed costs that each unit must bear decrease. Undoubtedly, management would welcome such productivity increases in a machine even under a constant machine cost per unit. But where people are concerned, the results may be unwelcome. People who were paid more than those in the rate-busting department are now paid less. Semiskilled workers may be receiving more than skilled workers or supervisors in the same plant. Since pay is a common status symbol in industry, the relative social standing of organization members is cast in doubt by changing differentials in pay. Workers in other departments feel threatened and can be satisfied only by some maneuver that re-establishes the

[6]In the considerable literature on workers' acceptance of managerial productivity goals, Chapter 3 in James G. March and Herbert A. Simon, *Organization*, New York, Wiley, 1958, probably contains the most thorough attempt to organize relevant sources of influence. William Foote Whyte, *Money and Motivation*, New York, Harper, 1955, is surely the most extensive treatment of the subject, containing numerous examples.

older, jealously guarded pay relationships in which even a few cents an hour may be fraught with social meanings of considerable importance.

Similar situations have developed in insurance companies under older contracts with salesmen. As business improved, successful salesmen could make considerably more than company executives. It became the practice for some companies to offer a private office and a title in exchange for the old, remunerative contracts. The Los Angeles office of a national firm at one time contained a sole holdout against the offer of a title in return for his contract. He was certainly the most highly paid individual in the office. His desk was located in what was essentially a secretarial and typist pool filled with young girls, probably as a mild punishment for his behaving too much like an economic man. The support that enabled him to hold out against company offers came from the informal organization. Strangers visiting the office were told his story in hushed and envious tones. It was rather like visiting an India where Ghandi lay in jail and no one knew the name of the colonial governor.

The worker who is relatively isolated from both the formal and the informal organization, as the assembly-line worker may be by noise and inability to move from his position or as the salesman may be by distance and the infrequency of encounters with others in the firm, is particularly susceptible to dissatisfactions that bear little relationship to pay.

A young salesman, after a very successful year selling to food stores for a national firm, made the following report:

> Don't get me wrong. I'm not fed up with the job or anything like that. It's just that I wonder. I've outsold everybody in the district who handles the kinds of accounts I do. But every time I sell more, they just raise my budget [quota]. The district manager gives me the old pep talk, but nobody above the district level knows I exist. One guy who couldn't sell anything started out with us. Then they moved him to national headquarters and he's already had a promotion.
>
> This job is not what you'd think. You know what I spend 80 per cent of my time doing? Moving cases and opening them, straightening stock. Just plain physical labor. Hell, I didn't spend four years in college for that. But the pay is good. I can't complain about the pay. They put me in for a promotion to product supervisor. But all that is is a fancy name for what I'm doing right now. I'll call on the same accounts and make thirty or forty dollars more a month.

I'd like to work for a smaller company, someplace where I could move ahead. Not now, of course; I don't know the business that well yet. I don't kid myself that I'm ready to manage anything yet, but in a few years . . .

It is not difficult to determine the nature of this young man's relatively mild dissatisfaction. He has fairly high status demands that are not being met by activities his job requires and will not be satisfied by high-sounding titles that lack reality. Insufficient contact with others at the levels he aspires to seems to him not only a temporary isolation but perhaps a permanent barrier to his social progress. His work performance is probably not impaired yet, but he has lost confidence that superior performance will get him to the levels he wants to reach in the next few years, in part because a fellow worker was given what he regards as a significant promotion (a job in the home office) apparently through inability to handle the salesman's job. The chances are very good that in a few years this young man will be hired away from the national company to become the assistant sales manager of a smaller firm where he will be more closely associated with the managerial personnel he wants to regard as peers, and where he will have the ability to direct others and initiate activities. And he may well accept a smaller salary than he is making at the time in order to take a job in which the social and personal rewards are greater. He is thinking vaguely now about taking graduate work, since education is the major path to vertical mobility. Of course he expects appropriate increases in income when he demonstrates managerial ability.

Mobility

Status improvement is not always sought by workers. An increase in status may be seen as a threat to a satisfactory life situation. Perhaps the most strongly resisted promotion is that from worker to foreman. A reasonably large number of workers recognize that they will not be happy in a job that sets them apart from their fellow workers and imposes upon them the unwanted role of leadership. Such persons frequently refuse promotion because the social loss, as they see it, clearly outweighs any economic gain. Whyte gives an excellent example of this kind of reasoning in the refusal of a promotion.

Well, I've been working for Jack for five years now and we have always got along good together. I just didn't want to make the change. I remember how it was when I was working for this other fellow. I was on edge all the time. Then when I would go home at night I would get in arguments with the wife and kids. It's different today. I get along good on the job and I get along good at home. It isn't worth eight dollars to me to make that change.[7]

The person who makes such a statement is, in all probability, the son of lower-class parents. His wife is probably from the same background. His education undoubtedly stopped with high school, even before graduation. His friends outside work are generally laborers like himself. If any of these social involvements had been different (such as middle-class parentage, or a college education), he might have accepted the promotion. If many of them had been different, he would have been seeking it impatiently.

Even those who are ambitious may reject promotions for social reasons unassociated with the work situation. Rejections of this sort are not uncommon when the promotion entails relocation. Nationwide firms find it increasingly necessary to move employees from place to place in the course of insuring satisfactory managerial succession or orderly corporate growth. While these movements, along with a high rate of interfirm transfers, have helped create the peculiarly homogeneous national subculture of the suburbs, the process of suddenly being pulled out of one social context and thrust into another is never comfortable.

Some elements of the working population are highly mobile, either because they generally move at the same times and to the same places that friends do (as is true in the aircraft industry or heavy construction where jobs follow contracts), or because they know that ready-made social contexts like their own exist in the areas to which which they are moving. Scarsdale, New York; Evanston, Illinois; and Palo Alto, California, are merely different places inhabited by a single social group, in which a fantastically large percentage of the people have common friends or acquaintances. And even where these are lacking, the common values, interests, and experiences make assimilation into local social groups easy for the newcomer.

But it should not be mistakenly assumed that all persons are reasonably mobile or that those who are will move anywhere for a better paying job — or any job at all. A person who might willingly

[7]William Foote Whyte, *Men at Work*, Homewood, Ill., Dorsey, 1961, p. 158.

take a promotion that requires his moving from the suburbs of New York to those of Los Angeles is quite likely to refuse one that would place him in Decatur, Illinois (a different sort of community) or Birmingham, Alabama (a different regional subculture). On a recent movement of its home office from New York to a small Ohio town, a fairly large corporation lost almost one third of the managerial and engineering staff that would have been required to move. And people at this level are generally regarded as among the most mobile.

Age strongly influences mobility. The young, especially those from 18 to 30, are apparently eager to seek out economic opportunity wherever it exists. But even this group does not have anything like complete mobility, nor is there much reason to believe that economic opportunity is more than one factor encouraging the degree of mobility that does exist. From farms, rural areas, and small towns youth tends to move first to the smaller, nearby city and then to the larger city — the smaller city providing a sort of social decompression chamber where the young can learn urban ways without departing completely from the small-town atmosphere. But to suggest that increased economic opportunity is the sole, or even major, reason for place-to-place movements among the young is probably a serious oversimplification. The glamor of the city and the opportunity to escape the social strictures of the smaller community are probably at least as important as economic considerations.

At some age or at some stage in the family cycle mobility decreases considerably. The birth of the first child, which may occur at an extremely early age, limits mobility. And even those families that move often as the husband climbs the managerial and salary ladder normally reach the point where being able to settle down to a single location outweighs financial considerations, either because moving itself is such a major social and physical effort or because family ties in the present community have become particularly strong. A major corporation with a set policy against firing high officers chose a transfer from New York to the West Coast as its first maneuver in attempting to force the resignation of a vice president. The theory was that his social ties and those of his wife and daughter were too strong to be broken for the difference between his regular salary and his prospective retirement pay. A variation of this combination of economic and social influence is suggested in the offer of a machinist to accept a job in Danbury, Connecticut, for twenty-five cents an hour less than he was currently making.

"My wife's family," he said, "lives in Norwalk, and I figure that Danbury is just the right distance away."

Social ties and custom become so strong that they may, on occasion, lead to behavior that is economically disastrous. Large numbers of people (primarily the middle-aged and the old) apparently prefer to face real poverty than to leave the bituminous sections of eastern Tennessee and West Virginia. The anthracite regions of Pennsylvania experienced deep depressions for a decade while perhaps the majority of the unemployed merely waited for economic opportunity to come to them rather than going out to seek it in the booming cities of Houston, Tampa, or Los Angeles. In more isolated trouble spots, such as Cairo, Illinois, the reaction is similar. No amount of economic hardship seems great enough to drive marginal farmers off the land, and most of the reduction in the agricultural labor force is probably the result of the children of farmers failing to replace their parents in that occupation.

The farmer may be among the very hardest of persons to force out for economic considerations, since he has in addition to his immediate social ties the support of some of the weightiest cultural values. He is independent, a property owner, and the property he owns is endowed with a special cultural magic, since it is land, the age-old symbol of independence.

Work decisions, from the acceptance of the first job to retirement, are all clearly influenced by a combination of social and economic elements that does not unravel into a simple system. The result is that any single career followed through its entire course may seem to be dominated by chance. Although it is largely structured by economic and social factors, individual and situational differences may seem to make the particular career unique — especially if it is one resulting in remarkable success. But social considerations are paramount in determining what opportunities will knock and how the individual will answer.

6 ▶

The Sale

     The basic event in a market economy is the sale. Economic policies and decisions are oriented either to past or to future sales, even when they are apparently directed toward reducing unemployment or modifying international gold movements. For this reason, sales executives are prone to contend that "Nothing happens until a sale is made." Such myopia is not uncommon among business practitioners, who, whether they be engineers, advertising men, personnel managers, or accountants, are likely to imagine that their own specialty lies at the very heart of the economic process. (In fairness, it is necessary to add that politicians, musicians, physicians, college professors, and housewives seem equally capable of viewing the sun in orbit around their earth.)

     A sale depends, of course, upon a host of prior events and of presumptions about the future. It does not rise out of some near-vacuum at the magic touch of the master salesman or at some inexplicable whim of the purchaser. The buyer and seller both operate within a larger context that includes the buyer's social and cultural background and the seller's, as well as their expectations. In a sense, the individual sale is merely incidental to certain broad cultural developments and levels of technology. The sales of automobiles in 1907, 1945, and 1963 were very different things because of cultural and situational changes.

     While it will be impossible to discuss the event of the sale without some reference to the larger setting within which it occurs, the principal focus of this chapter will be upon the immediate situation within which the buyer and seller find themselves, their relationships with one another, and the particular leverages they apply or misapply.

     If the sale has no unique economic significance, it is certainly critical to the economic process as we know it. Yet the context within which the sale occurs is not neutral, but is characterized by non-economic pressures. People meet and talk, form opinions, vacillate and consider, seek advice and reject it. While the results may be economic, the process is social.

Perhaps one of the great discoveries of the modern, commercial world is that sales can be accomplished within any normal social relationship — even within pure mimicries that disregard social reality completely. There simply is no single, approved role for buyer or seller. And the social ingenuity of both can make the sales situation a fascinating game or a frightening experience, simply because society has granted the participants the greatest possible latitude in this particular kind of encounter.

The sales situation was not always so unrestricted. Certainly at one time in the western world, the seller and buyer were almost always in the servant–master relationship — or a close facsimile of it. Peasants were not buyers, and the nobility or their representatives purchased from merchants or individual producers. There was no need for a slogan declaring the customer always right, since he had the armed men to prove his case and little reluctance to use them. The mimicry of this servant–master relationship remains today, especially in the "better" retail stores, restaurants, and service establishments. But it is often a cold and cynical mimicry that hovers on the edge of insult, on the look-out for customers who are not of the expected class. This "traditional" relationship of buyer and seller may explain in part the extreme reluctance many young salesmen show when making a call, since this places them in a situation in which they are essentially powerless (as they see it) and subservient to the whims of an unknown master.

It might be argued successfully that some element of the servant–master relationship remains in all normal sales situations, since the seller is interested in making the sale and willing to adapt to a reasonably broad set of buyer demands. If the argument is successful, it is also trivial. With persons of all types in the role of buyer and with the role of seller subject to continual commercial analysis and innovation, the variety in sales situations becomes too great for emphasis of single elements. And in some states of the market the buyer pleads for goods or services.

Yet the temptation to seek generalizations that will hold is great. One of the most plausible generalizations is that the social distance between buyer and seller cannot exceed certain limits. If the sales situation is a social situation, it would seem that persons of diverse social background would not enter it as buyer and seller. Yet it is clear that in particular situations customers prefer to buy from someone of a higher or lower class than their own. Charles Roth tells of a salesman who attempted to dress and talk in the manner of the farmers who were his prospective customers, only to find that they preferred to deal with equipment salesmen who were obviously successful.[1] In one southern city upper-class families drive all the way across town to purchase barbecued meats from a lower-class Negro who is something of a "character" and who makes the best barbecue in town. One upper-middle-class young man who worked briefly as a waiter discovered that his friends disliked going to the restaurant where he was employed. Apparently they preferred to deal with waiters whom they could regard as belonging to a class lower than their own.

Some national companies feel that it is important to use salesmen of the same general subculture as the people they call upon. Their sales staffs in the South are made up almost entirely of Southerners and their branch offices in New England generally have New Englanders working out of them. But this matching of the subculture of buyer and seller is increasingly ignored. When a new shopping center opens in Austin, Texas, the staff selling space to retailers may come from some development group in Boston or Baltimore.

An organization selling products to chemical engineers may use chemical engineers as salesmen. But this reliance on the special relationship that exists among members of a particular professional group seems appropriate only when the items being sold require highly technical exchanges between buyer and seller. No one would suggest that nuclear physicists would do the best job of selling shoes to other nuclear physicists.

Since there is no single set of roles appropriate to buyer and seller, even in the sale of a particular kind of product, the most effective role must be developed within the context that exists. The knowledgeable buyer may feign great innocence, essentially forcing the seller into the role of expert. The lower-middle-class clerk may put on airs of hauteur that cause an upper-middle-class customer to accept the clerk's expensive tastes. The roles played in the sales situation are not necessarily closely related to social realities.

[1]Charles B. Roth, *My Lifetime Treasury of Selling Secrets*, Englewood Cliffs, N. J., Prentice-Hall, 1957, p. 154.

In some extreme cases the roles played seem to make little sense, except for their relative success. In Chicago, shortly after the second World War, an Italian restaurant achieved great renown for the behavior of its waiters, who insulted customers, refused to give them what they wanted, substituting chicken cacciatore for ravioli or chianti for burgundy as the spirit moved them, and generally behaved as though the customer were a barely tolerated intruder. Some women who would file for divorce if their husbands treated them similarly seem to enjoy being bullied by a hairdresser or interior decorator.

Like many temporary or brief social relations, those between buyer and seller may simply mimic well-recognized, firmly established social situations. The hairdresser who bullies the middle-aged matron is obviously playing old-fashioned father to her little girl. Both recognize the pretense and play it as a sort of half-game. In other cases the mimicry may be intended to confuse the other party, as is the case when the encyclopedia salesman pretends to be an educational expert — even going so far in his opening statement as to suggest that he has an intimate knowledge of how the housewife's son or daughter is performing in school.

Of course, there are limits to the extent to which either salesmen or buyers can assume roles successfully. The department store sales clerk who presumes intimacy and calls the customer "dearie" is more likely to lose effectiveness than gain it. In this case the lower-middle-class clerk fails to establish the aura of intimacy desired simply because she uses a term that the real intimates of the upper-middle-class shopper would never use. Social role playing requires both knowledge and ingenuity if it is to be successful. In the hands of experts the selling role may be far removed from any reality, although one may ask of a role that has been accepted for a lengthy period by a particular buyer and seller whether it has not, in fact, become a new reality. The industrial salesman who feigns friendship on his first call may well become a close friend of the buyer he calls on regularly over the years. Certainly the new life insurance salesman leans first on the real social relations that exist, attempting early sales to friends and acquaintances before he begins to build up the larger list of potential customers. And as he joins clubs, takes on committee assignments, and widens his circle of acquaintances, it becomes difficult to determine where social realities end and role playing begins. In all probability there is a mixture of reality and mimicry in most sales situations that neither party can assess fully. Nor does the degree to which the situation mimics other social relations have to be considered cynical. The buyer is as important as the salesman in the development of roles and seems frequently to prefer to deal with someone other than a factual, impersonal salesman. In fact, sales managers slurringly refer to such salesmen as "order takers."

Roles are liable to change with different products, in different physical surroundings, and with different participants. For this reason, there is no really satisfactory set of divisions for the analysis of the social influences in the sales situation. Yet there are certain broad differences between the range of possible roles available when one businessman sells to another in industrial selling and those available when a salesman sells to a consumer.

The Sociology of Retail Sales

There are a number of different methods of carrying out retail sales. In some, the social interaction between buyer and seller is either absent or minimized. Vending machines, mail order sales, telephone sales, and even the sales made in some self-service stores are characterized by relatively little buyer–seller contact. Of course, this does not mean that social influences are unimportant in such sales — they may be as vital as is the case when a woman buys a particular breakfast cereal because her children insist upon it. The social relations between buyer and seller however, are relatively inconsequential (although a supermarket manager or his cashiers may be of some importance in determining what store a woman will shop in).

Social interaction assumes its full role in retail stores that have sales clerks and in house-to-house selling. The basic difference between these two situations (the house-to-house salesman relies in part on the fact that once in the door and seated he becomes a quasi-guest) makes buyer–seller roles appropriate in one of these situations that cannot be maintained in the other.

The retail store is quite likely to have relatively strong class characteristics. That is, the customers of a store tend to be of more or less the same socio-economic class. Abercrombie and Fitch is not designed to get the patronage of Davega customers; Marshall Field's does not expect to attract all the customers that shop at Sears Roebuck. Differences are not merely price differences, although these may be important in limiting customers. The nature of the merchandise, the way in which it is advertised and displayed, the décor of the store, all aid in the selection of shoppers. As Pierre Martineau says:

> In a study of department stores and shopping behavior, it was found that the lower-status woman is completely aware that, if she goes into high-status department stores, the clerks and other customers will punish her in various subtle ways.[2]

There are at least three general classes of furniture stores. The first deals in what the trade knows as "borax" and sells largely to lower- and lower-middle-class consumers. The second handles more fashionable furniture but emphasizes relatively standard items. The third specializes in high-fashion merchandise, often giving decorator services on rooms and finding special fabrics. Obviously, the social role of the salesman must vary with the merchandise and the customer. In the first type of store, the salesman is apt to be forceful, dynamic, and just a bit brusque. He may play the part of the tipster on price or be obsequeous. In order to speed up the customer's reaction, he may rely heavily on the role of busy businessman who is impatient with a relatively unimportant sale. He is quite likely to let the customer know that he has superior information and taste and that his word should therefore be taken as law on the matter. But he is not completely limited in role. He can be a helpful, friendly confidant with considerable success, if he can allow himself to be so. Unfortunately, he is not usually far enough removed from his customers socially to treat them with dignity. He recognizes that his own status is limited by the store he works in and the customers he waits on, and he has a difficult time resisting small social triumphs that are as likely to hurt the possibility of a sale as to help it. The customer, often unsure of quality and usually uncertain of his own taste, finds it difficult to withstand the value system of the salesman in determining what is a good buy or what is fashionable.

The salesman in the second type of store is much more likely to be friendly, treating his customers as equals, deferring to their opinions. He is probably less certain of his own ability to judge what is in good taste than is the salesman in either the high-fashion or the "borax" store, because a number of his customers look down on the kind of furniture he has in his own home. Like the salesman of "borax" he is

---

[2]Martineau, Pierre, "Social Class and Spending Behavior," *Salesmanship: Modern Viewpoints on Personal Communication* (Steven J. Shaw and Joseph W. Thompson, Eds.), New York, Holt, 1960.

no expert in styles and fashions. But he cannot readily play the expert or insider, because his clientele may have superior knowledge. He is much more likely than the "borax" salesman to talk about matters unassociated with furniture, discovering what the customer's job is and discussing events of common interest. He wants to be liked and makes a point of finding some common ground with the customer. It is almost impossible for him to use pressure, since his role gives him neither the social position nor the *expertise* from which to exert leverage. In a sense, he is not really a salesman at all, but a member of the Junior Chamber of Commerce helping another member or his wife look for an appropriate chair or lamp. His patience is great, since he is dealing with friends rather than customers. His manner may change abruptly when he is called upon to wait on a member of the lower classes, but, since he is really playing himself, he is equally likely to remain helpful and patient — although he will not usually attempt the overtures of friendship that are his stock in trade with members of approximately his own class.

The salesman in the high-fashion shop generally knows furniture construction, fabrics, and current fashion better than do his customers and has complete confidence in his own judgments. If a lower-class customer enters the store by mistake, he will be warned off rapidly, but subtly. Unlike the salesman in the middle-class store, the high-fashion salesman does not attempt to establish casual friendship with the customer. His talk is all of furniture and decoration, with emphasis on the esthetic rather than on the practical elements of construction. He wishes to be regarded as a specialist and makes his *expertise* known. He is willing to play any of a number of roles with the buyer: he may play instructor to the intelligent but uninformed customer, he may accept the buyer as fellow connoisseur, he may play the role of fashion arbiter to the uncertain. His customary ploy is to show off pieces in which the customer is not interested: "Of course, this fabric wouldn't be right for your living room. But isn't it exciting?" He does not sell furniture so much as visual effects. In a sense, he is Pandar arranging a love affair between the purchaser and nine feet of brocade-covered couch. It is difficult for him to resist the temptation of effeminacy in his enthusiasm for line and color. The buyer must, obviously, live up to the salesman's taste and is placed under strong pressure to do so. Certain pieces that the middle-class furniture salesman would write up without question become "impossible" for the purpose considered, and only the strongest-minded buyer can insist. When this happens, the high-fashion salesman may simply refuse to allow his customer to make such a mistake. Or, if he is less of the martinet and more of the flatterer (roles unsuitable for the sale of lower-class furniture to lower-class customers), he may suddenly discover that the customer has hit upon a very subtle and unusual combination which he can make work by the addition of a pillow or two, a change in the piping, or a new lampshade.

It is obvious that in normal social usage, the customer already owes the store salesman something for taking up his time and for being shown the stock of items in which he has expressed interest. Those with relatively weak egos can hardly resist buying something, simply because it is expected of them — and may select in desperation the least unsatisfactory of an inadequate list of items. This social pressure exists whatever the nature of the buyer–seller relation. The nature of the unspoken additional pressures exerted by the salesmen in the three types of furniture stores might be described as follows:

> Borax — "Look, I'm a busy man. Make up your mind and let's get it over with."

> Middle Class — "Look, I'm a nice guy, and I've tried hard. Won't one of the things I've shown you do at all?"

> High Fashion — "This is an absolutely perfect combination. If you don't buy it, I'll know that you either can't afford to purchase in this store or are completely lacking in taste."

Of course, these are only some of the more obvious kinds of social pressures that can be brought to bear on consumers through the more usual buyer–seller relationships in certain kinds of stores. Other relationships can serve as the basis for other types of influence. Individual salesmen and store executives are on the constant lookout for particular sales roles and situations that will increase the amount of influence and make sales more likely. Possessed of considerable ingenuity, they have discovered an almost endless variety. Two of the more recent are involved in self-service operations and the sale of automobiles.

The self-service operation is really designed to remove the social pressures that exist in every buyer–seller relationship. It is recognized that the mere presence of the salesman prevents large numbers of persons from looking at things that they are not seriously interested in, because of the presumed social obligation to buy unless the product is in some way unsatisfactory. Knowledge that this pressure will be present apparently keeps numbers of buyers out of stores when they have no specific purchase in mind or drives them out after they have made the particular purchases that were planned in advance. Lack of such pressure in the self-service store allows the shopper to look around at his leisure, incurring no social debts to store owner or salesman. Such leisurely perusal of merchandise seems to do as good a job of suggestive selling as many experienced salesmen, and accomplishes more than the mediocre sales clerk at less expense. With the presence of other customers, cashiers, and sales persons who help in the completion of the sale of merchandise the casual shopper has selected, a number of social influences remain. But the major social pressures of the continually present salesman are avoided.

The complex ritual of the automobile sale, on the other hand, has created a completely new setting, as fully stocked with good guys, bad guys, and side characters as a television drama. In this playlet, the customer is allowed the protagonist's role, and the fair-minded dealer even provides him with a personable crony to help him combat the heavies of the piece: the sales manager and the appraiser. In this never-never land the sales manager and the appraiser are always hard pressed by the good guys, who plot coups and exert pressures on them. The salesman gallantly rides forth to get $50.00 more out of the appraiser by pointing out that the car is a real cream puff. Then salesman and buyer put their heads together to see whether they can get the sales manager to throw in a radio at cost and power steering for nothing. The salesman tries and partially succeeds, and obviously is a bit bloody from the encounter. "He tried to throw me out of the office when I mentioned it," he reports proudly to the customer.

In the process, salesman and buyer are likely to become real buddies; first names are passed back and forth, the kind of fishing story that is normal among intimates may change hands. Seldom is the drama finished in a day. The salesman calls to report his latest progress with the sales manager. And finally, when the exact deal the customer will accept has been determined, the dealer himself may step in and make the grand gesture of acquiescing.

The enormous advantage of creating an in-group (salesman and purchaser) and an out-group (sales manager and appraiser) places the customer in a position where he is much more likely to trust the salesman (after all, they are fighting this out side by side) and feel a real responsibility to him. At the same time, the dealership is protected from any hard feelings, since the enemy is an unseen sales manager or appraiser who is rigorously trying to show a profit for the warm-hearted dealer, who would probably give cars away if he were permitted.

The social role of salesman as the buyer's friend and agent is not unique to the sale of automobiles. It occurs in the sale of real estate, where the realtor by keeping buyer and seller apart can play the same role with both, and in many industrial situations. In fact, the role may become reality under some circumstances and the salesman may actually serve the customer better, and be closer to him socially than to the organization that pays his salary or commission.

Retail sales that take place in the customer's home are quite different, sociologically speaking, from those completed in a retail store. The principal difference is that the salesman takes on some of the aspects of the guest once he has been admitted and is seated. (The housewife scurries about picking up papers or children's toys in much the way she does for any other unexpected visitor.) In addition, the noncommercial surroundings make the occasion something more of a social and less of a business situation. The buyer in the retail store can easily break off negotiations at any time to leave, especially when the offered products do not quite serve his need. But it is almost impossible for the buyer to end the sales presentation in the home; one does not demand that guests leave but waits until they are ready to go. On the other hand, automatic pressures to buy are lessened. The salesman's time is less valuable because he offered to give it rather than having his assistance sought in the retail store.

Sales talks are longer and more leisurely and take place in relative privacy. Beauty Counselor operates on the assumption that many women, who would like to use the newer cosmetics but have never learned how, will not approach a sales person in a store with requests for information for fear of looking inadequate. In their own homes, approached by a woman of approximately their own age and social class, they will welcome information on eye shadow and the more exotic forms of make-up. Personal selling in the customer's home can become particularly effective when only the saleswoman and the housewife are present trying out new cosmetics. The housewife may look in the mirror, but she must still rely in large measure on the only other person present to evaluate the effect; thus the saleswoman becomes a social leader in the capacities of both advisor and judge.

Part of the reward the customer receives for purchasing is the sales-woman's approval, as is true in many sales situations.

Door-to-door selling is one of the few circumstances in which salesmen regularly adopt the role of supplicant. It is completely natural. Societies and smaller social groups are, after all, mutual protection associations. And one of the strongest dictates of virtually every known society is that the strong protect the weak, that the rich help the needy, that the mature support the young and the aged. In an industrial and commercial society with strong values on enterprise, initiative, and trade, sheer beggary is generally inappropriate. But the combination of beggary and sales gets strong social support. The blind beggar sells pencils or provides music rather than asking for gifts. The Girl Scouts sell cookies. About the only major organized efforts to embody this social relationship between buyer and seller in a commercial enterprise (unless one insists on regarding a number of charities as commercial enterprises) is the magazine-subscription sales organization. The boy or girl who plays the seller is taught not to talk about the magazines he is selling but about the number of points he will receive in some contest and how badly he needs them.

The role of the salesman as supplicant would be relatively un-important, if it were not resorted to elsewhere. Almost any retail salesman is likely to emphasize his need to make the sale, with the rather sure knowledge that a large number of potential buyers will consider this a partial reason for making the purchase. This aspect of the basic economic decision to buy is so contrary to any existing economic model that it is generally disregarded. But society is a coopera-tive enterprise more than a competitive one, and the role of supplicant is broadly or subtly played in sales of all sorts, both to consumers and to businessmen.

The salesman calling on the retailer asks, "Couldn't you take an-other case? It's been a bad week, and I really need this sale."

The giant airframe company says in effect to the Air Force, "We've laid off more than ten thousand men since March. If we don't get work soon we'll have to close down the entire Hanover plant. We need the contract to modify those planes."

The lumber broker calls the contractor. "I have seven carloads of two-by-fours that I have to get rid of. Can't you take a couple of them for me?"

No one would suggest that the role of supplicant is the most successful selling role, but it is used occasionally in many situations, and sometimes it adds enough social weight to the economic balance to complete a sale.

Stanley Home Products has developed one of the most successful selling techniques embodying (rather than simulating) the relatively intimate, face-to-face group. The sale of the products takes place at a party in the home of a member of the group. The hostess is not a Stanley representative, although she receives points, good for the purchase of Stanley products, for her cooperation. The number of points she receives depends upon sales made at the party, the number of guests who attend, and the number of guests who agree to give such a party themselves. An initial number of points is given for holding the party. Guests get refreshments supplied by the hostess and small gifts furnished by Stanley. They also participate in games organized by the Stanley representative, who is trained to make the party fun; and winners receive Stanley products as prizes. The Stanley representative herself is an enthusiastic socializer who acts much like the ordinary social leader of such a group (getting games under way, helping the hostess plan refreshments, making sure that everyone is thoroughly a part of the activity). Tupperware is sold in much the same fashion.

Women who attend such parties normally feel obligated to make at least some minimal purchase. Enthusiastic party-goers may withhold purchases of certain products for the next party. The commercial representative actually becomes a member of the group when parties are held with some frequency, and members pass the valuable role of hostess from one to another.

It is quite easy to become appalled at such mixtures of selling and social obligation if one does not realize that virtually all sales have a social content and that the social return for both the hostess and the guests can be great.

None of this is intended to indicate that consumers make foolish purchases because of the social leverages utilized by salesmen. Rather, it is intended to indicate something of the diversity in sales methods, all of which have social contexts. The salesman can affect the role of parent giving stern or helpful advice, of intimate suggesting how the peer group will react to a particular purchase, of supplicant seeking aid and placing the buyer in the role of benefactor, of panderer, of social leader — the list is endless.

It might be supposed that industrial sales and other sales to businessmen would not be characterized by so much social interaction — that they would be based more on the calm consideration of price and quality, specifications and materials. There is little evidence that this is true. Relationships between buyer and seller are of tremendous importance, often simply because price and product characteristics are identical or nearly so for many industrial products. The salesman selling steel or sugar or flour is, after all, dealing with a highly standardized product and he can hardly be expected to prove that his sugar is better, or even different, from that offered by others.

The Sociology of Business Sales

One study of industrial salesmen showed that on the average six calls were made by the salesman on the same potential customer before the first sale was made. This kind of statistic calls for speculation. If the product being sold was really good enough to purchase, why did not the acute business buyer purchase it after the first presentation? One possible explanation is that in business, one normally does not purchase from strangers and that after approximately six calls, the salesman is no longer a stranger.

One of the outstanding flour salesmen of the thirties seldom called at prospects' offices. He usually made arrangements to meet them at his golf club. A par golfer himself, he was a tolerant and patient instructor. His customers enjoyed playing eighteen holes and picking up a few pointers that saved them strokes as much as they appreciated the praise he lavished on them for a fine, natural swing or a good eye. They enjoyed the luncheon or the supper at the club after the round was over. And they bought a great deal of flour.

The luncheon meeting, the nightclub tour, the hospitality room are standard items in the sale of products to the businessmen, whether they be store owners, manufacturer's purchasing agents, production engineers, or higher executives. The simple-minded see the process as commercial bribery or some kind of tax-evasion plot. The more accurate explanation is that businessmen are not really much different from the leaders in primitive societies who preface their discussions of practical affairs with a round of the pipe or the trading of gifts. All are rituals during which strangers can size up one another, discover some of the other's interests and personal idiosyncracies, and determine whether he is someone with whom it is sensible to deal — whether he can be trusted.

The extent to which the ritual meal of buyer and seller is truly a social rather than a business occasion is indicated by one salesman's surprise at the unbusinesslike behavior of architects.

> You take a purchasing agent or executive out to a meal — he eats and drinks everything in sight and talks about women and baseball. Architects? They take the blue-plate special and talk shop.[3]

The ritual first meal of buyer and seller does not necessarily include the discussion of business matters. The salesman who begins to discuss his product during cocktails is obviously a boor or socially naive. The least he can do is to wait until coffee or dessert, when the Mandarin he is entertaining may ask: "Now, how do you think this coupling of yours can speed up our construction contract?" Equally probably the invitation to talk business will not come until both have returned to the customer's office.

It would be a mistake to believe that the salesman always pays for the meal. He undoubtedly will if he has approximately the same rank (or status) as the buyer. A salesman usually buys the lunch of a purchasing agent. But if the salesman has a luncheon appointment with a vice-president or the president of a company (it would normally be a small to medium-sized concern or the protocol would be seriously upset), it is quite probable that the executive would pick up the check — in fact he might specify that they eat at his club where the salesman could not possibly pay.

Of course, the ritual meal is not possible in all contacts; a salesman usually has to make more than two calls per day, and many of the businessmen who make purchases are pressed for time. The retail store manager or owner cannot normally indulge in more than the briefest social amenities. Harold Schafer, president of Gold Seal Company, explains his attempts to establish himself with retailers as follows.

> When I called on a store, if the man who owned the store was washing windows, I started helping him wash windows. . . . If the storekeeper was unloading a truck load of flour in back of the store, I helped him unload flour. In one lumberyard I helped unload a couple hundred sacks of cement. In one store I helped wash shelving with soap and water and put on display competitive merchandise. I helped several men sweep

[3]William Dudley Hunt, "Selling to One Group of Idealists — Architects," *Salesmanship: Modern Viewpoints on Personal Communication* (Steven J. Shaw and Joseph W. Thompson, Eds.), New York, Holt, 1960, p. 247.

their floors on my early morning and late evening calls. A lot of people will say this is not the right approach, but believe me, it works.[4]

What Harold Schafer means, of course, is that his approach is but one of the social roles that a salesman can use in establishing his relationship with store owners and managers. If he were selling to large department stores such as Macy or large chains such as A & P he would find that the purchasers were not of the type who could be approached by rural American neighborliness. The fact that a lot of people say it is not the right approach merely demonstrates that there is no single role for salesmen, even when they are selling to other businessmen. But there is an initial stage during which the salesman must establish his relationship as friend, acquaintance, fellow Dodger enthusiast, or whatever. Businessmen simply do not buy from strangers.

The pseudo-intimacy between buyer and seller is often established rapidly. First names are traded, often at the first meeting when it is between those of approximately the same status level. The sexual or scatalogical story is passed along, not so much because of any all-pervasive interest in sex, but because such stories are normally told among intimates or close friends and become symbolic of a closer association than the mere handclasp. The normal relationship between buyer and seller when both are businessmen is one of peer-group intimacy. It may merely be a mimicry of that relationship, or it may develop into a real friendship, since the same salesman may call on the same buyer with frequency over the years. The salesman is more than merely maudlin when he says: "But it was really the start of a beautiful understanding friendship that lasted for years, to the mutual benefit of both sides."[5]

But familiarity, acquaintanceship, or pseudo-intimacy is merely the social prerequisite to business sales. It will not, in itself, assure a sale or provide the social pressure that may strongly influence one. It is the salesman's certificate of *bona fides* and little more. Even a relatively close relationship between a salesman and a single member of the buying institution may have little effect unless the relationship

[4] J. M. Hickerson, "Successful Sales Techniques," *Selling: Its Broader Dimensions* (Taylor W. Meloan and John M. Rathmell, Eds.), New York, Macmillan, 1960, p. 304.

[5] Cason Rucker, "Basic Selling," *Selling: Its Broader Dimensions* (Taylor W. Meloan and John M. Rathmell, Eds.), New York, Macmillan, 1960, p. 317.

is at a relatively high executive level. The reason for this lies in the complexity of business organizations and the many kinds of social relationships that exist within and between organizations.

Organizations of any size normally have a number of people who can influence purchases directly or indirectly. The owner of a garage may be sold on a particular oil absorbent largely because of friendship with a salesman. Sales will probably not continue, however, if the mechanics who work in the shop have preferences for another oil absorbent — or simply resist using any. The office manager may find that it is difficult to purchase a particular brand of typewriter, because the salesman has been unpleasant to one or two secretaries, or because a secretary prefers another machine. The owner of a motion picture theater may refuse to rent a particular film because his wife is sensitive to the comments of her friends, who disapprove of a particular actor or actress or of the salacious advertising that goes with the picture. The purchase of an installation in a manufacturing plant usually receives the attention of production engineers, plant and maintenance engineers, the purchasing department, and the comptroller's office or accounting department — and usually more than one person from each of these areas is concerned. Some industrial salesmen report that most sales are made to production engineers, but that it is tremendously important to maintain good relations with the purchasing department or the engineers' requests will not get through.

Imagine the situation in a medium-sized petro-chemical company faced with the problem of purchasing a digital computer. The IBM salesman is a long-time friend of the comptroller, helped him set up the payroll and inventory system, and has for some time served as an excellent source of information on computer applications. The production chief, who wants the computer for the analysis of processes and the development of on-line control systems, roomed at Massachusetts Institute of Technology with one of the engineers who helped design the Control Data Corporation model that is being considered. In fact, his reason for starting the project was a conversation with the friend at a recent IRE convention. Two members of his engineering staff have close acquaintances who work for Remington Rand. General Electric is a moderately heavy user of the company's plastics division products. The vice-president in charge of marketing worked for the Radio Corporation of America five years ago and has many close friends there. One member of the board is also a member of the board of a medium-sized electronics company that has just begun to produce a line of three general purpose digital computers.

There is no attempt to make this an unusually complex situation. Businessmen move from company to company, attend industry-wide or professional meetings, have wide acquaintanceships in numbers of organizations. Institutions themselves develop relationships, both positive and negative, with suppliers and purchasers, financial institutions, and the like. And most of these connections become very like the social ties that make the prospect say to the insurance salesman: "I have a brother-in-law in the business; and, if he can give me the same policy at the same price, I'll have to take it from him."

Of course, with so many complex relationships among businesses and among the people in businesses, it is too much to expect that all of them will pay off in sales. And it would be fanciful to believe that many organizations make decisions to take clearly inferior installations, raw materials, fabricating parts, or whatever merely because of some social relationship. But judgment of quality is often difficult. No two computers manufactured by the companies mentioned above would be exactly the same. Prices would differ, storage methods might differ, speeds of computation would probably differ, capacities would probably differ. No machine would be exactly right for the job; and no one in the purchasing company would know just what was needed beyond certain general limits. Undoubtedly several of the computers would have some characteristic more desirable than those of others. It is under just such circumstances that some of the social connections would take effect, probably subconsciously. One can almost hear the comptroller saying: "IBM has been in this business a long time, and we know we'd get the best service we could ask for." And one can almost hear the engineer in charge of operations answer: "This isn't an accounting machine we're talking about."

The internal organization of a corporation is a dynamic society in which power shifts slowly or rapidly from one locus to another. With no general agreement on which installation is really best for the purpose, it is natural for each of the points of influence to attempt to get its preference accepted and to block the preferences of others. Most internal struggles of this sort are carried with reasonable tolerance for diversity of opinion and willingness to compromise. Characteristically, most individuals concerned are responsive to factual evidence and are reasonably willing to consider any logical argument that will help clarify the picture. But, in the end, few institutional decisions are equally agreeable to all parties. Someone's point of view prevails, usually because more power is enlisted in its support than is available to alternatives. It would be impossible here to discuss the complexities involved in lining up power behind a certain proposal, but they are the normal politico-social activities probably described better by novelists than by economists, sociologists, or students of business. C. P. Snow's *The New Men* and *The Masters* and Cameron Hawley's *Executive Suite* do thorough and imaginative jobs of detailing the way in which forces are brought to bear on a problem. The fact that novelists tend to write only about the complex struggles that attend decisions of major consequence is related to their desire to maintain reader interest. Any careful observer recognizes that many decisions of little importance often involve the same sort of contest.

The more routine the sale, the fewer persons will be involved in the decision and the more influential the relationship between a single member of the buying institution and a salesman will be. But the reality of the interpersonal relationship is often clearest when the salesman and a representative from the purchasing company get together over a drink to commiserate with each other because some other supplier got the contract.

It would be a mistake, of course, to think that a salesman selling to businessmen is always cynically trying to make a sale. Typically he spends much more time with his customers than with members of his own company. He builds social loyalties to them that will often cause him to refuse an order if he does not believe the purchase to be a sensible one for the customer. He is quite likely to side with his customers against his own company, expecially in matters of credit and shipping schedules. Faulty merchandise makes him as irate as it does the purchaser. So clear is this tendency of the salesman to represent the purchaser rather than his own company that counteracting this is one of the main purposes of sales meetings and conferences where sales staffs are brought together periodically. Some companies routinely shift territories and change assignments simply to prevent the growth of overclose relationships between individual salesmen and their customers. The preferred relationship, from a corporate point of view, is the interinstitutional relationship rather than the interpersonal one — although it is obviously not possible to maintain the former without establishing reasonably strong personal friendships as well.

But intercorporate relationships of some strength do develop between the buying and selling companies. Corporations have their favored contractors, management consultants, package manufacturers, raw materials suppliers, and the like, much as individuals have their family dentists or lawyers or grocers. That is, corporations are simply not neutral toward one another as economic theory suggests. General Foods does not purchase the bulk of its glass containers from Anchor Hocking because of better prices or better delivery schedules or better credit terms than it can get from Hazel-Atlas or Owens-Illinois. Its primary reason for dealing with Anchor Hocking is a long-term relationship, based in part on personalities, in part on a history of good service, in part on intercorporate familiarity. As most industrial salesmen know, it takes strong arguments to get a corporation to give up its regular sources of supply, even for a single sale. And the arguments must be presented within some meaningful social context. But this is not so difficult to establish as the young salesman often thinks.

There are strong forces tending to bring persons together during the sales call. Once moderately friendly relations are established, the salesman offers particular social advantages to the buyer that are probably not available elsewhere. The salesman is in the unique position of knowing the buyer's business and other similar businesses at least moderately well. Therefore he can talk shop in a sense that the buyer's purely social acquaintances cannot. In addition, he is outside the buyer's company and is not in a position to help or hurt the buyer's career, is not competitive with him for promotions and raises. The result is that the buyer often feels a degree of freedom in discussing matters of major interest to him that he feels with almost no one else who is equipped to understand them. If looking for another job in the industry, he may find that the salesman knows of openings. If searching for an assistant, he may discover that the salesman knows of someone who is dissatisfied where he is currently working. It is not unusual for a buyer and a seller together on the town to indulge in confessions and activities that neither would participate in among members of his own company. Obviously, the social ties between such individuals become strong. And recommendations from either to the other may take on values that suggestions from other sources would not.

Hierarchic Protocols

It is impossible to talk about the social relationships between buyers and sellers in business without discussing the hierarchic protocols that dominate and direct these relationships. In general, the salesman calls upon persons who operate at approximately his own levels in the buying organization. The salesman calls on a design engineer or the assistant to the head of the purchasing department. He establishes his good faith with these individuals, and this suffices for the accomplishment of relatively routine sales. But one man is simply not capable of bearing the full representation of a supplier of even moderately important equipment.

When one company considers the purchase of fabricating parts from another with which it has had no previous dealings, a number of practical considerations, such as productive capacity, ability to meet specifications, and assurance of continuous operation, are difficult to evaluate. A normal way to provide the needed assurances to both buyer and seller is a plant visit by a group of representatives of the buying firm. Probably the salesman himself would not set up the visit. It would normally be preceded by a meeting between his sales manager and the production manager and some of his staff at the buyer's place of business. This would be primarily a social function, determining whether a full-scale meeting were worth while to both parties. If conditions seemed favorable, a mass visit would take place, with persons from the various departments of the buying corporation visiting the supplier. It would not be unusual for this to involve a party of twenty or more people, who would begin by an inspection of the plant and attendance at a general presentation of company operations and capabilities. This would usually be followed by a lunch. All visitors and their opposite numbers might lunch together, or the affair might be broken down into smaller groups of like interest and similar status. The presidents of the two companies would probably not be satisfied until they had lunched together in reasonable privacy, perhaps with one or two top aides in attendance, perhaps alone. After lunch, specialists from the purchasing corporation would pair off with those persons from the supplying company who could give them the detailed information they would like. Productive machinery and inspection systems would be carefully examined. Design engineers would explain their concepts in full. The financial and managerial control of the organization would be discussed with reasonable thoroughness. It is not unlikely that a return visit would be made by representatives of the supplying company to the major plant of the purchasing corporation, ostensibly to learn its problems and processes first hand. There are practical reasons for such visits and countervisits. Many are technical; but equally important is the understanding of the personalities involved. And the outcome may depend as much on the "kinds of people" involved as on any other single factor. This kind of diffuse, over-all judgment is, in essence, a social judgment, hardly different from the kind of judgment one makes about new acquaintances. And the process is almost identical with the social process where two families visit each others' houses: children play with children, women examine kitchens and compare house furniture prior to the establishment of real family friendships.

And just as a disagreeable teen-ager or a husband who tells bad jokes may prevent further association between families, so a corporation president who is highly atypical, a chief of production who has particular professional prejudices, or a marketing vice-president with "unsound" political or economic opinions may prevent the development of an intercorporate seller–buyer relationship.

The following account is a reasonably thorough description of the various meetings and get-togethers involved in the sale of a major installation.

While there was no particularly close relationship between the East Coast power company and a large equipment manufacturer, the latter's salesman had been calling on the company for several years. He was reasonably well acquainted with about eight members of the power company's engineering department. While taking two of them to lunch one day, he received information on a possible sale to the power company. This involved the construction of a new power-generating installation of unique character recommended by members of the engineering department and a finance executive. Together they had discovered that some generating equipment received little use — that it was in operation only about four hours a day for twenty-five days in the year when demand was at peak. Their conclusion was that the construction of a cheap installation to handle the peak loads would allow the company to delay construction of first-class generating equipment with a consequent saving of considerable size. Regular suppliers had attempted to talk the power company out of the project, and showed no interest in handling the job on a simplified, low-cost basis. The equipment manufacturer's salesman returned to his own company to determine its willingness to undertake such a project. While he ran into resistance because of the novelty of the installation, he received support from his sales manager, who had heard about a similar operation in the Midwest. The equipment manufacturer began design work on the project, and its salesman began calling on the power company at an increased rate, approximately once a week. The persons he talked to were primarily those in the power company's engineering department, but he also made several calls on the manager and assistant manager of the operating department, since they would have something to say about the new installation. He also talked with the member of the finance department who had been one of the originators of the plan.

The power company decided not to use its usual engineering consultants on the project, largely because it was so different from the usual installation and because a vice-president of the power company ran into an old friend at an industrial conference. The friend, now the vice-president of an engineering consulting firm, had worked side-by-side with the power company vice-president in a third corporation some years previously. His firm was chosen to consult on the project.

The newly selected consultant and the equipment manufacturer worked out a rather interesting design incorporating a marine boiler to strip costs as far as possible, although the equipment manufacturer was already well along on a design incorporating a commercial boiler. After several months and repeated meetings among various members of the three companies involved, a presentation was made at the power company's office. Present were some fifteen persons from the power company representing engineering, operations, and finance. The engineering consulting company sent its chief mechanical engineer, a design man, and a regional representative as well as its vice-president. The equipment manufacturer sent its salesman, its regional representative from the West Coast (the engineering consultant's location), and a sales specialist on marine boilers. The presentation was an all-day affair. The engineering firm made the morning presentation; the equipment supplier made the afternoon presentation. Most of the twenty-two persons involved attended the luncheon. Absent from the meeting was the senior vice-president of the power company despite arrangements for his presence. His absence indicated at least that he did not regard the project as major, perhaps that he did not wish to become involved in a possible dispute between engineering (which was enthusiastic about the project) and operations (which had been lukewarm at best and had already made a number of objections known to the equipment manufacturer). All specific objections of the operating department had been met with design modifications prior to the presentation.

It is also significant that no one of reasonably high executive rank was present from the equipment manufacturer. In all probability this absence suggests that the appropriate executives of that company suspected that the project would fail or were simply unwilling to become involved with something as questionable (unusual) as the project.

After the presentation, the power company attempted to make a decision. Engineering was enthusiastic; operations had serious doubts. Neither had the power to force its decision on the other, and the higher executive who could force one or the other to back down had withdrawn from the struggle. The result was a compromise. New designs would be asked for incorporating a commercial boiler rather than a marine boiler, since there had been no tested use of the latter in such an application. Further, the company would ask for bids on the job rather than dealing with a single supplier.

During the period of redesign, the equipment manufacturer attempted to establish a better understanding with the operations department of the power company. Seemingly, the effort was too late. Neither the manager nor his assistant could find the time to visit a similar, nearby installation until the salesman chartered a plane that cut the trip down to a short morning's work. After the visit, a two-hour lunch demonstrated that the operations people were somewhat less pressed for time than they had contended.

Prior to submitting its bid, the equipment manufacturer asked to give a final presentation that would last a morning. Only five or six people from the power company attended; the more important participants were all absent. Clearly, the project was rapidly losing support, although the power company engineering department was still enthusiastic and strongly favored the bid of the equipment manufacturer. It was the lowest of four bids on the job, two of which were not seriously considered for one reason or another. One of the rejected bids came from a regular supplier. It was thought to be merely a courtesy bid, since that supplier had strongly suggested that the low-cost installation not be built.

Prior to the date on which the decision on the bids was to be made, the project had been reported by the trade press. A number of power companies expressed interest in similar installations. The publicity had other effects on the project. A nearby power company with excess capacity re-examined its rate structure on power sold to other companies. The senior vice-president of the power company originating the project had formerly worked for the company with excess capacity and continued to play in a golf foursome that included some of his old colleagues. They twitted him about building a stripped-down plant to handle peak loads and suggested that he buy power from them instead. In quick succession the senior vice-president, who had previously withdrawn from negotiations, re-entered the picture and rejected all bids; the company with excess capacity lowered its power rates and wrote a contract with the original power company to supply it during periods of peak demand; and the engineering department commiserated with the equipment manufacturer's salesman.

It is hardly necessary to point out that the economic objectives of the originators of the project were achieved within a social context. The equipment manufacturer got its chance because its salesman had spent years building up friendships in the power company and because regular suppliers essentially refused to take the project seriously. The basic contest was not between salesman and buyer, but between the two departments of the purchasing company. This disagreement could hardly be economic in any usual sense of the term. The two decisions that were completed — the contract for the delivery of power and the hiring of an engineering consultant — both took place between friends of long standing. The final decision may have been the most economic solution to the problem of handling peak demand. But whether it was or not, it was, like all buying decisions, strongly influenced by the social forces brought into play.

7 ▶

The Nature of
the Business Organization

A great number of the major economic decisions of our world are made by organizations rather than by individuals. Perhaps it would be more accurate to say that these decisions are designed to serve organizational goals rather than personal goals. The terminology is difficult, because normal usage is metaphoric. One says that General Electric is building a new plant or that Du Pont has developed a new synthetic fiber or that Whitaker's drug store has put in a luncheon counter. It is presumably recognized that these things have been planned and accomplished by people working within an organizational framework, but the picture of Du Pont as some great intelligent beast with its brainpan lying athwart the state of Delaware and its limbs casually brushing the Andes or the Mountains of the Moon is not easily dislodged.

But neither the great corporations nor the small proprietorships are unitary except in the studied inaccuracies of the law. They are organizations, not organisms. To view them as monolithic may sometimes seem appropriate, but it involves an essential misunderstanding of their nature and ignores the real miracle of their existence. Commercial organizations have no wants and no needs of their own. The wants are all those of members of the organization, the workers, managers, owners, suppliers, and consumers. It is possible, of course, to think of the organization in the more limited sense of owners, managers, and workers. But this restricted concept of the organization makes it difficult to explain its equilibrium and is, for this reason, losing favor among students of business.

Each of the groups gives something to the organization: time, services, money, or the use of money. And each expects something in return: money, products, or services. It is important to the existence of the organization that each participant restrict the wants he expects the organization to satisfy directly. Only through such a tacit understanding by the worker that the organization will demand only some level of skill and effort and that it will return to him little more than wages (leaving most of his wants to be satisfied outside the organization); or by the stockholder, who specifically does not demand that the organization supply his affectional or associational wants (or in fact anything much beyond what he regards as a satisfactory monetary return), can the organization remain viable. While some of the terms of this understanding are conscious, even legal, others are often unrecognized until the events to which they are appropriate occur. One employee may warn his immediate superior several weeks before he leaves the job, because he perceives that as a part of his unspoken contract. Another may simply fail to show up for work, because he does not regard notice as a part of the understanding. It is axiomatic that the specified and unspecified conditions of the understanding are dynamic, changing over time as the various participants bargain with one another directly or indirectly.

Corporate and Personal Goals

In order for the firm to function as an organization through which useful exchanges of services, effort, and money can be made, it must have both profits and longevity.[1] It is the goal of administration to maximize profits insofar as this is possible without jeopardizing the continued existence of the firm as an effective organization. Most economists and businessmen agree that this is the rational goal of the firm, although many may want to modify the wording or elaborate the statement. It is only in terms of a rational goal that organizational efficiency can be discussed.

Because of differences in the nature of the social contracts involved, it is advantageous to regard the organization as stretching out in all directions around an administrative center. Near the periphery, the contract is weak and the flow of information is limited. Neither the individual worker, stockholder, nor supplier is likely to

[1]The exciting new concept of organization slack (Richard M. Cyert and James G. March, *A Behavioral Theory of the Firm*, Englewood Cliffs, N.J.: Prentice-Hall, 1963) suggests the need for revision of the concept of profit maximization as the rational goal of the firm, implying that alternative disposition of corporate resources not required to hold the organization together may be more sensible.

know much about organizational plans or problems except in the most general terms. Nor do any of them freely inform the administrative center of even those things that might be of considerable value to the firm.

The consumer who finds a new use for a product is little inclined to let management know of this use. Banana flakes were fairly commonly used as a baby food well before either the manufacturer or retailers discovered the fact. For this reason neither appropriate promotion nor convenient placement on food store shelves was possible.

The stockholder seldom feels committed to use the firm's products, give management advice, or more than superficially glance at the annual report. He may even resent having to sign a proxy statement.

The worker who discovers easier ways to carry out his assigned task generally keeps the discovery secret since he does not regard work simplification as a part of his contract. Nor will he often cooperate with time-and-motion studies designed to increase productivity. According to Whyte:

> Occasionally, an inexperienced worker under the observation of the time study man becomes so nervous that he cannot help speeding up. Experienced workers avoid this error and pride themselves on their ability to slow down while still appearing to work fast.[2]

One would not want to fault the efficiency of the firm simply because the nature of social organization is such that all participants do not contribute as fully as they might. To believe that such levels of contribution are really possible is to make the error of thinking of the organization as an organism with a single set of values, cognitions, and wants rather than as a collection of individuals with diverse interests. To gain greater cooperation and involvement of all members might well demand the expenditure of more resources than the results

[2]William Foote Whyte, *Men at Work*, Homewood, Ill., Dorsey, 1961, p. 105. Of course, the consequences of this sort of activity are not uniform. Whyte continues, "The experienced time study man is not fooled by such maneuvers. He knows that the workers are trying to fool him, and therefore he makes allowances for the play-acting he observes." This is rather similar to the way in which a department manager may overstate his budgetary needs only to have his action counteracted by the fact that the budget committee assumes that he has overstated those needs.

would warrant. And a full flow of voluntary information from peripheral areas could well swamp even the largest and most capable
administrative staff. At the same time, it is worth noting that Western culture does not support the firm completely in its attempt to
behave rationally, and that both economic theory and cultural history
encourage the limited commitment of peripheral members to the
objectives of the firm.[3]

There is another essentially social limitation on the firm's behavior. The organizational patterns are adapted to specific activities,
and neither patterns nor activities can be altered easily. Just as there
are "sunk" costs in capital equipment, so there are sunk and present
activities. For instance, one might imagine the difficulties involved
in converting the Chicago Bears of the National Football League into
a baseball team, should baseball offer greater financial rewards. Not
only would a large number of personal skills become inappropriate,
but new modes of cooperation and interaction would have to be developed. The disorganization of team, coaching staff, and general
management can readily be imagined. Yet the change required is
not so enormous as it may seem at first blush. Baseball is a familiar
sport to most of these superbly conditioned and remarkably coordi-
nated young men, many of whom could easily have become professional baseball players.

In combination, the "sunk" costs or inconvertible resources make
it difficult for the firm to take advantage of even a moderate number
of the economic opportunities that are present. The whip industry
of Westfield largely died with the advent of the automobile and only
a few firms were able to shift successfully into furniture manufacturing
or the production of carnival supplies. The subcultural difference
between a research-oriented glass firm like Corning and a production-
oriented organization like Anchor Hocking is not something that can
be wiped away by a few administrative orders or a revised budget.
Administrative competence is not so much at issue as administrative
style, organizational values, and modes of behavior. Current management cannot maximize profits, then, with any certainty when maximization implies functional changes of great magnitude. It is not
surprising, then, that the powerful railroads did not participate in
the profitable opportunities offered by bus, truck, or airline trans-

---

[3]Economic theory would seem to suggest that the member minimize his
contribution, and Western cultural history is full of individualistic values that
conflict with the requirements of corporation life.

portation. Nor was it unexpected that the automotive manufacturers should play such a small role in the economically rewarding airframe and airplane engine industries.

An A.T.&T. cannot be expected to rush into the commercial development of all the inventions and discoveries of its Bell Laboratories, or even all of those that promise greater than average rewards. So a Texas Instruments may be allowed to seize much of the profit opportunity of some new product such as the transistor. Economic theory has uncovered no natural mandate on the pace or direction of innovation for organizations or even whole economies.

To rule innovational activities out as inappropriate for the limited purpose of this discussion does no more than emphasize the incompleteness of the rationality concept. It remains to point out its partiality as a model of the day-to-day activities of the firm.

Formal and Informal Organization

Commercial institutions have a formal organization that is hierarchic, culminating in an individual, such as a president, or an executive group such as a board of directors. The various positions existing within the organization have stated interrelations suggesting some of their functional characteristics — just as the table of organization of an infantry company indicates something about the chain of command, the power structure, and some of the functions of particular members and subgroups. On the other hand, human organizations are never mechanical in the sense that an organizational chart or a blueprint is. Thus, a president or department manager of an organization almost never functions in the same way as his predecessor or successor. The Attorney General under Kennedy does not have the same powers and functions as the Attorney General under Eisenhower or Harding. The differences in powers and functions is in part a reflection of the differences among individuals, but to a larger extent it is based on the differences in the relationships among individuals. Informal relationships exist and develop within the formal organization. As the formal organization is structured to conform to certain functional demands of the firm, the informal organization is structured to satisfy some of the wants of the individuals and groups who man the institution. It is far too easy to imagine that the demands of the firm and these wants of individuals that are reflected in the informal organization are conflicting — in large measure they are corollary or mutually supporting.

In fact, the informal organization can adapt itself to pressing organizational needs without demanding action from the formal organization. An erroneous order is acted upon as though it were correctly given where the informal relationships involved are favorable. The formal organization is bureaucratic and stiff, slow to make decisions and slow to react. This fact is recognized by most employees, and informal short cuts are commonly developed. Suppose, for instance, a design engineer making a model of a potential product discovers that he does not have the machinery with which to finish a particular part. He may have only two courses of action available through the formal organization. First, he can requisition the necessary machinery through his department in a process that requires the approval of the department head, a special committee, and the comptroller's office. After the approval is granted, the purchasing department may be required to request that suppliers submit bids, review these bids, and then place an order. The entire process may take thirty days. Second, he may be able to have an outside organization make the part for him. This, also, may require various formal approvals and other actions that will consume about the same amount of time. If he has good informal relations with someone in production, on the other hand, he may be able to go directly to a friend there who will slip his job into the regular production schedule, despite the fact that there is a standing order against using production machinery for any other purpose. Both of the persons involved would explain that the action was in the company's interest since it saved at least a month in the completion of a working model without slowing down production at all.

Time-saving and cost-saving actions of this sort are common in business. How many millions or billions of dollars they save a year is unknown because employees at all levels tend to regard their informal connections and activities as private matters.[4] Nor does anyone know how much is lost through the workings of the informal organization when the engineer wants to repair his fishing reel, when the department covers for an absent member, or when the stockroom

[4]Simon says, "It probably would be fair to say that no formal organization will operate effectively without an accompanying informal organization." (Herbert A. Simon, *Administrative Behavior* (2nd ed.), New York (Macmillan, 1961, p. 148.)

is used for a crap game or an amorous adventure. It is simply the nature of people, whether they wear the title of machinist or president, to believe that they are the best judges of what is or is not in the interest of the organization and what does or does not conflict with that interest. Of course, the informal organization will not tolerate every variety of excess and its policing is remarkably effective. But the crap game or the Friday afternoon golf match indulged in once as a mild aberration may become an occasional event, a normal occurrence, and finally a right protected by the informal group as meticulously as though it were part of a written contract. In this sort of process, the executive has the advantage since he can claim to be thinking matters over or refreshing his outlook while on the golf course. By the simple expedient of picking his foursome with reasonable care, he can make the affair a matter of "pure" business and even pretend that he dislikes the obligation. The worker indulging in the crap game and those who protect him admit that the action is not in the interest of the organization and justify it in some much more roundabout fashion.

A portion of the social contract is that managers and professionals expect to find pleasure on the job and business considerations mixed into their pleasure, but that workers will separate the two in appropriate segments of the day. In general, this clause has been accepted by informal groups, often so thoroughly that the formal organization is powerless to determine the lunch hour for certain classes of people, and can merely acknowledge or ignore the times established by the informal organization. So, in a particular office, junior executives may take no more than forty-five minutes of their allotted hour, while those at other levels feel obliged to stretch theirs out as befits their status.

The incidence of administrative peccadilloes naturally varies greatly from organization to organization. And the economic consequence of such unproductive activities is unknown. Surely, there are many instances where a few words dropped on the fifteenth tee or the deal consummated during the second, or even third, hour of lunch have justified an executive's salary for a full year. And there is no evidence on hand to suggest that the most businesslike shop is always the most productive shop. Matters of this sort are worth mentioning only because they support the conclusion that members of an organization will normally attempt to increase the number of personal wants the organization satisfies and will tend to explain their behavior in terms of organizational goals. Further, these explanations will often become a part of the folklore of the individual corporation, the industry, or perhaps the entire business subculture.

The Disposition of Power

Since decisions are generally made through bargaining and sanctioning processes, it is desirable to examine the way in which power is disposed among participants. The formal organization states authority relationships, although not unequivocally. The manager of the payroll division may request that a clerk prepare a particular report that requires going to certain back files, but a painter from maintenance may for several hours keep her out of the room in which the files are stored. Such small events can rapidly lead to the involvement of several levels of management in an attempt to discover where the power to settle the affair resides. Of course, the location of the appropriate formal authority will be clear, but the parties involved will be reluctant to call in a vice-president to handle a dispute between a clerk and a painter. The result is that other moves will be attempted first. What is being sought is either an existing informal relationship between someone in the payroll department and someone in maintenance who can order or influence the painter or a person in the payroll department who can quickly establish such relationships. It may be that all that is needed is an attractive girl with a pleasant manner. Or the office manager of the payroll department may know the foreman under whom the painter is working. In general, the solution to the problem will be attempted with the smallest amount of authority possible — and the least display of power.

Power realities are largely hidden from the new employee and are only incompletely understood by the veteran, since they are largely informal and those who employ power normally learn to use no more than is necessary for the task at hand. Some foremen run their crews, others are essentially run by them. But where personal relationships are good, it may be difficult to tell which is which.

Power is not only largely subterranean; it has other diverse characteristics. Power may be highly specific; it is probably never really general. It may inhere in information rather than in people. Always it relates to a particular situation. And it is in continual flux.

Every member of an organization has certain particular powers reserved, at least for the moment, to him alone. It might be argued that much of this power is of a negative sort, since a task that it takes thirty people to accomplish may be blocked or delayed by one. But much of it is positive. A particular individual may be able to get information from the shipping department in half the time it takes his own immediate superior. Another may be able to get a certain typist to turn out work with greater speed and accuracy than anyone else can persuade from her. Often in managerial decisions this kind of particular power relates to the special *expertise* or information of the individual. The tax expert may simply point out the influence on taxes, or the engineer can flatly state the impossibility of carrying out a particular project. And either may suggest an alternative method that will make the operation possible. But even chance bits of information can deliver the momentary power of the expert. The advertising cub who knows that an agency has lost a competitive account may, in effect, determine the firm's choice of advertising agency. The person who knows exactly how far production is behind may strongly influence the rejection or acceptance of a contract.

While there is no implication that information is always accurate or that identical information is equally powerful no matter who holds it, the nature of informational flow within an organization strongly influences the distribution of power. The formal communications network is partial, and with good reason. No one could possibly read all the reports, memos, policy statements, and the like generated by even a moderately sized corporation. Routinely, the persons to whom such information is sent are highly selective in what they take account of. Beyond this, published information that is pertinent to many situations may be voluminous, and always differentially available to the participants in any decision. Lastly, the informal communications network is highly selective. In one organization, there may be no reasonably direct informal channel from accounting to marketing. In another, there may be several open lines of high capacity.

The informal information channels differ from the formal in a number of ways. Information carried is of a different sort, not in the sense that informal channels do not often transmit the same essential information that may be carried by formal channels, but that they carry additional information that is never mentioned in memos or reports. Much of this different information refers to interpersonal relationships, motives, and aspirations. Matters of this sort are of major importance in business decisions, since they are used to discount or give extra weight to the viewpoints of participants. (Nothing is so disturbing in a conference as the inability to determine why a particular person holds a particular point of view.)

Informal channels are usually less reliable than formal channels, carrying more misinformation. This is not to say that formal channels are invariably accurate. It is not at all unusual for the informal communications to provide the only realistic account of events or managerial motives, since they are normally rationalized when they are reported formally. A large class of formal messages are met with anger or laughter because of their inaccuracy or because they naively confirm the suspicions and beliefs that travel the informal channels.

Perhaps no distinction between these channels is more important than their directions. Informal channels naturally follow the informal organization. This means that information travels most rapidly among people who see each other frequently and who are on the same corporate level. Informal information that passes up or down the authority structure is carefully screened. One does not tell his secretary everything he tells his boss or his boss everything he tells his secretary. The manager, like the betrayed husband, is often the last to learn about something that affects him most directly. By comparison the formal communications generally follow lines of authority and are most effective in what is shown on organizational charts as a downward direction. Only the simplest kinds of factual information flow upward with any readiness or accuracy. The result is that for many purposes each managerial level is essentially isolated from those below. And high executives occasionally complain about their inability to discover "what is really going on," in the way they could at earlier points of their career in frank discussion with their peers.

Of course, information or *expertise* ultimately has only that power which participants in the decision-making process are willing to grant it. The statistician of twenty years ago often found that his most valuable contributions to the understanding of a problem were not given serious attention, largely because management was unsophisticated in statistical techniques and regarded such considerations as too "theoretical." While persons who discount experts and theoretical considerations still inhabit the executive suites, a growing number seems overimpressed. The statistical analysis may receive far more weight than other types of information, not because it is more pertinent but because it is statistical. And, as everyone knows, when the statistical manipulations have been carried out by computer, their persuasive powers are multiplied.

In an organization in which information is not common property its possession implies power. To a large extent both the informal and the formal organization see to it that the information that has power implications is available to appropriate individuals. For instance, the department head, who normally has informal relations with others operating near his level in the organization, is generally provided with information about plans and policies that is not available to others below his position in the firm. Beyond this, he normally sits at the information center of his own department receiving reports, all of which are not passed on to superiors and all of which have not been made available to subordinate members of the department. Every executive sits in such a key information center, which is at once the source of his formal power and a reflection of it. The close relationship of power and information is so clear that the first signs indicating a loss of power may well lie in the discovery that an inferior has been given bits of organizationally important information that could only have come from above or that his superiors are in possession of information about his own area that he has not yet given them. Some of the most important information available within an organization concerns the changing power relations themselves. These power relations are dynamic and incompletely understood by all parties. Some decisions are likely, therefore, to be based upon apperceptions of power realities. Since perceptions are different from realities, it is not unusual for an individual to think that he has either less or more power than he actually possesses at the moment or to misunderstand the power wielded by others. But people at management levels are generally expert at analyzing the power structure involved in any decision-making process. They might even be referred to as students of the dynamics of power, always sensitive to its present location and the probable shifts it can take. Since, however, power is never the overt issue in a decision-making situation, many of the powers available to the participants, will probably not be brought into play. And the superficial aspects of the situation will seem to indicate that logical analysis and economic considerations are paramount in arriving at a solution. Not only is the power structure but slightly exposed during the decision-making process, the diverse interests of the participants are generally well disguised. The presumption of self-interest is, of course, commonly accepted. But self-interest is neither simple nor isolated. It tends to operate through group identification and loyalties. And, to a considerable extent the values, modes of behavior, and perceptual biases of the individual are derived from his social location within the organization. The process implies both conscious and subconscious elements. Dubin apparently emphasizes the conscious elements in the following statement.

> In some respects, clique conflicts within modern large-scale organizations are inevitable. A large number of capable individuals compete for a diminishing number of jobs, the higher they go in the organization. This may make the need for amassing clique support in order to move upward almost an imperative for driving and highly motivated executives.[5]

Simon and March seem to suggest the subconscious in the impersonality of some of their remarks, such as, "Rules originally devised to achieve organizational goals assume a positive value that is independent of the organizational goals."[6] In any case, long association with particular groups and activities normally leads to a more or less bizarre set of values that makes it possible for the trucking industry to advertise: "If trucks stopped for 72 hours, so would you!" Charles Wilson undoubtedly believed that what was good for General Motors was, in general, good for the United States, whether he said it or not. A real estate commercial heard frequently in Austin, Texas, used to begin, "Buying a home is the most important decision you will ever make . . ." The nature of this sort of myopia is closely related to the particular social loyalties the individual develops.

References of Loyalty

An understanding of the tangle of loyalties within the social fabric of the firm is necessary to any sensible discussion of its activities. Most individuals within the firm are members of a large number of groups and institutions, all of which command a certain amount of their loyalty. What is available to the firm may be great or small; however, since work makes up a major portion of adult life, the total loyalty available to job-oriented groups is normally large. Social commentators frequently suggest that it is too large in the United States — especially among executives of all ranks. But job-oriented loyalty can be of several sorts. A simplified set of categories might

[5]Robert Dubin, *The World of Work*, Englewood Cliffs, N. J., Prentice-Hall, 1958, p. 395.
[6]James G. March and Herbert A. Simon, *Organizations*, New York, Wiley, 1958, p. 38.

be: work-group loyalty, departmental loyalty, company loyalty, and professional loyalty.

Work-group loyalty is generally paramount in lower-level jobs. It is centered on the people one works with every day. One's behavior is shaped more by what John expects, what Charlie wants, what Helen requires, than by other and more abstract levels of consideration. Virtually all work groups (even at the general-officer or board-of-directors level) have this sort of loyalty to a primary, face-to-face group. As one gets above lower level jobs, persons tend to have a longer and larger view of the world, the firm, and their own relationship to both. Junior executives may have work-group loyalty — may, in fact, behave much as anyone else would in the same situation. But they are actually more reserved in committing themselves to the work group. They do not, after all, intend to spend many years on the same job or with the same people. Their loyalty can seldom be as personal or as deep as that of the individual who can anticipate spending much of his life in the same shop or office. The junior executive's relatively intimate relationships with those he deals with day-to-day are characterized by friendliness but limited commitment.

Departmental loyalty is common to all levels of work, but is perhaps strongest among the supervisory and low-level managerial employees who will work in a single, specialized area for long periods of time. The bookkeeper who will never become a comptroller, assistants in the credit department, traffic personnel, a number of workers who will remain salesmen or who will spend their lives in production, develop loyalty to the first level of abstraction above the work-group. The nature of this loyalty, since it is to an abstraction, is somewhat different from work-group loyalty. It is more likely to affect the general values of individuals rather than their direct relationships to other persons. The entire warehouse crew is likely to be largely responsive to these first two levels of loyalty: the warehouse and the work group stretch to the horizons of their active awareness. The fact that it is a General Motors, General Foods, or General Electric warehouse is known and has some place in their thinking. But any real loyalty to the parent corporation is essentially meaningless, since all behavior is carried out in terms of what it means in warehousing procedure or what Charlie and Jack think and do. In one corporation the warehousing system was such that the storage and withdrawal operations cost more than the value of the item being stored — but this was of small concern to the warehouse personnel, since they felt no real loyalty to the organization as a whole. They were merely concerned with operating the warehouse properly, not with corporate profits (or the proper management of the storage function).

In small companies, company loyalty may be essentially what departmental loyalty is in larger ones, simply because all operations are visible. But in larger (and even middle-sized) operations, true company loyalty can be a difficult kind of thing to create — at least its strength may well remain minimal. Neither the morale builders (such as IBM's song sessions) nor institutional advertising (such as that of U. S. Steel or A.T.&T.) is likely to create it in individuals whose group values and understanding do not easily run to such levels of abstraction. The union, symbolized by a single leader (especially when he is a Dubinsky or Lewis), is a much more concrete object for loyalty than the corporation — which is seldom very well symbolized by any executive officer. In fact, the managerial requirements of the commercial institution and the undemocratic system of their appointment generally make it inevitable that few corporation presidents will command the personal loyalty that political parties and labor unions enjoy or will serve well as corporate symbols. The corporation is forced, therefore, if it is to be run by an increasingly professional group, to remain essentially impersonal. Personality, in the traditional leadership sense, can be given only slight emphasis as a criterion for executive selection. In general, there are two approaches to the widespread absence of strong company loyalty. The first, which promises small success because it runs counter to the workaday world in which the individual experiences the company, is the attempt to use the media of mass communications to persuade workers that the giant corporation is really a sort of tight little family that can be symbolized in folksy terminology. The other is to utilize the increasingly technical paraphernalia of administration to develop the coordination that informal social organization can accomplish only in work group or department.

The fourth type of loyalty is to the profession (that term being used in its broadest sense). The activities of the accountant, lawyer, personnel manager, statistician, engineers of all sorts, the market researcher, economic analyst, and a host of others are steadily becoming more professional in nature. The ultimate loyalties of these workers may reside in the standards and techniques of their professions as these develop. Such loyalties tend to be coldly passionate, impersonal, and less flexible than other loyalties. It may make sense to consider what is in Charlie's best interests in comparison with the interests of a department. It makes almost none to consider the relationship between Charlie's interests and the techniques of standard cost or linear regression. To increasingly professional people, making the "right" decision for the company may be of much less importance than arriving at the decision in the "right" way. (These two considerations may seem the same, but with these technical areas far from perfected, they may be quite different.) While loyalty of this sort exists predominantly in staff positions, there is a marked trend toward professionalism in all areas of management. The tremendous growth in size, capability, and influence of colleges of business would suggest that line positions are being rapidly professionalized as well.

Most members of the firm have loyalties of all four types, but these may differ greatly in degree. Even at higher executive levels one may find persons who are primarily loyal to their own work group, those who are primarily loyal to the company, those who carry strong departmental loyalties with them even after they have been promoted above the departmental level, and those whose paramount loyalty is to some external professional group. This means that policy and decisions are made within incomparable contexts. The discussion of a promotion may find one person favoring the leading candidate largely because he worked with him closely at some time in the past. A second may be against him because he comes from the wrong department ("We need someone with a solid production background for this position"). A third may favor him because he has demonstrated strong company loyalty. The fourth may exclaim, "But he hasn't even the vaguest notion of what a standard error is."

Under such circumstances it is easy to understand why many conferences seem incoherent or muddled. Not only is there disagreement over the solution to the problem, there are even greater differences in concepts of what the problem really is (what are its important and what are its trivial aspects). But even if its results seem sometimes nonexistent, the conference serves a number of important functions that may be described as primarily social. It brings together in a face-to-face group persons who have no other (or few other) personal relationships, creating an informal group that would not otherwise exist. The full play of values and powers that exist within the group become understood in the way that family relationships become accepted. Any given member of the group can then determine in advance the likelihood of a particular decision being made and can shape his own proposals for group approval. Perhaps more important, such familiarity makes some decisions and policies unnecessary. At least certain decisions become routine and can be made by a single member of the group with sure knowledge that he has group approval. And certain informal policies need never be stated. (Unstated policies are often the clearest, most thoroughly complied with, and most dynamic — changing slowly in adaptation to current circumstances.)

Beyond this, reasonable degrees of conference-group loyalty and tolerance develop. Decisions relating largely to operations within a certain area may be essentially placed in the hands of one conference-group member alone. This sort of tolerance may hold even for occasional pet projects that other members of the group neither fully understand nor approve. In other cases, a member may not push for a decision that he believes proper for the organization simply because he perceives and respects the doubts of other members. The decision-making group itself must remain viable as a social group, and a reasonable level of permissiveness is often the most readily available insurance of viability.

Thus far, the discussion has centered around the organization of the firm in order to explain the setting within which decisions are made. While it is clear that the organizational context is not one which exerts unremitting pressures toward profit maximization on members of the firm, there are characteristics of the profit goal itself that suggest difficulties in its pursuit.

The Context of Corporate Decisions

Unfortunately, the goal of profits is not a simple one, since profits derive from a coordination of diverse activities whose costs are normally understood in only the most general terms and whose contributions to profits (past, present, or future) is even less well specified. The result is that various units and individuals within the organization do not agree on the activities that would lead to the achievement of corporate goals. To oversimplify, a company that is operating at little or no profit may take one of two general courses to create profits: it may increase sales or decrease costs. But neither of these is a satisfactorily specific objective unless supplemented by a moderately detailed program by which sales are to be raised or costs lowered. In general, increased sales are achieved by such measures as changing the product, adding a new product line, increasing the advertising, or increasing the size of the sales force. Decreased costs can be achieved by laying off employees, buying cheaper raw materials or parts, introducing more efficient production or other systems, and so forth. From this it is obvious that some persons might recommend increasing the size of the research staff at exactly the time that others recommend curtailing its activities. Some might propose a study of production costs while others call for a study of consumer preferences. There are always a reasonably large number of activities not being carried out that might help in increasing profits. At the same time, the relative efficacy of these various activities is beyond objective measurement. The result is that most decisions made within an organization are made under the condition of uncertainty. This becomes a key factor in the operations of the formal and the informal organization, since it opens the door to those groups and individuals who, knowingly or unknowingly, project their own values as the legitimate interests of the organization. Avery's preference for liquid resources long dominated the post-war decisions of Montgomery Ward, not because it obviously led to profit maximization but because he was able to prevent other sources of corporate power from combining to support contrary points of view. His dominance of economic decisions depended largely on his ability to develop a supporting social system, rather than on evidence that profits were being maximized.

There are many examples of situations in which obviously wrong decisions have been made largely because of social influence of one sort or another. It is almost inevitable in a subculture that virtually worships modernity and efficiency that a number of firms would purchase computers because they represented the ultimate in these values rather than because of a careful analysis of just what a computer could contribute within the organizational set-up. A southern railroad had a general purpose computer installed and hired two programmers without having the first idea of what kinds of problems could be solved. Management hastily called in a group of college professors and asked, in effect, "Now that we've got this thing, what shall we do with it?" A number of banks discovered belatedly that automatic bookkeeping systems were uneconomic in institutions of their size, and in some cases the new installations did nothing but gather dust for months.

The new sales manager of an electronics manufacturing company failed in his job simply because he thought too much like a sales manager. The particular company was in difficulty because it had been selling custom equipment on which it could not show a profit. Salesmen in the firm had refused to understand that they were adding to the company's difficulties by looking for easy sales rather than profitable ones. In fact, they commonly boasted of writing up contracts for equipment that the engineering staff "hadn't even thought of yet." Having been briefed on the situation and organizational capabilities, the new sales manager was still unable to conceive that his job was not to increase sales. During his first few months on the job he personally wrote several million dollars worth of contracts on which the company lost several hundred thousand dollars, since he consistently sold what customers wanted in hopes that his company could produce it profitably. The fact that he was able to convince management to accept the contracts he brought in was due, in part, to the disturbed power situation in which virtually no member of management felt that he had the full confidence of the owners.

The ways in which social considerations become entwined with the economic is particularly clear in corporate policies and decisions on pay and promotions. The model of efficiency suggests that pay should be based either on the labor market or on the individual's contribution to profits or on some combination of these criteria. And the policy on promotions would clearly be that the most able should be given the job. There is little evidence that corporations operate in this way.

The large firm generally states the rates of hourly workers in ranges. For one job category the rate may be $1.85–$1.97, for another it may be $3.05–$3.20. Both the range for a given job and the difference in rates between jobs have important social meaning. Even the narrow range of ten or twelve cents an hour makes it possible for the firm to indicate something of the worker's standing in the organization when the job can be learned in a few hours time. The new employee works at the minimum rate for the job. After three to six months he will be given a small hourly raise, indicating that the firm is satisfied with his work and making him no longer a "greenhorn" on the job. Older men who have been with the firm for a longer period of time will receive the top rate for the job, giving them some tangible evidence that they are not crudely lumped with anyone who happens to have been around for a few months. It is not necessary that the older hands outproduce the newer; their higher wage rate is a social symbol rather than a measure of their greater contribution to profits. The difference in rates between jobs has a similar function, describing the skill level or relative importance of job categories. Whyte suggests the difficulties that arise when pay differentials between jobs are not related to social status in the plant.[7] And Warner and Low make it clear that these status relationships can be maintained over long periods after the relative skills involved in the original ranking have been changed by the introduction of new manufacturing processes.[8] Obviously, the reason for maintaining an outmoded status relationship is to prevent the disrupting influence of frequent status changes as the character of jobs is influenced by technological innovation. Tradition is seemingly a sufficient basis for some distinction in salary rank.

At executive or managerial levels pay is, in considerable measure, honorific. Almost everyone is familiar with the extensive symbolism of class that characterizes the business organization. Corner offices outrank side offices. Offices with windows outrank those without. At some class or status line carpets or water carafes become standard equipment, with more expensive carpets, carafes, paintings, or paneling marking the subtler distinctions from one level to the next. The key to the executive washroom has become the subject of an endless series of jokes and anecdotes.

Relatively little attention, on the other hand, has been given to the honorific nature of executive pay — perhaps because pay is such an important criterion of status both within and without the business organization. The department manager's salary increases annually more as an expression of faith and as a reward for loyalty than through any conviction that he contributes more to profits each year. Commonly the president is given a raise whether company profits are up or down. Of course, the manager is paid more than the people he manages no matter what their relative skills or their contributions to profits. In recent years there has been an occasional reversal of this gradient, especially in research departments where the talented chemist or physicist may be of far greater importance than the administrator immediately superior to him on the organizational chart. But even in such circumstances it is still normal to pay the manager the

[7]William Foote Whyte, *Men at Work*, Homewood, Ill., Dorsey, 1961, p. 118.
[8]W. Lloyd Warner and J. O. Low, *The Social System of the Modern Factory*, New Haven, Yale University Press, 1947, pp. 105–106.

higher salary for what must be regarded as organizational purposes. Nothing would, in the end, be more disruptive to the commercial enterprise than an attempt to pay people what they are worth to the firm or on the open market at the moment. Any such rational attempt to reward efficiency directly would undermine authority and make business little different from the jungle from which it is so far removed.

In essence the promotion system seems to be a compromise between locating the most capable managers and assuring the security of all. Demotions, in the literal sense, virtually do not exist, since the managerial class, like all upper classes, protects its own. Career sequences become relatively clearly established within the firm. The draftsman need not aspire to the position of vice president in charge of production, since there is no appropriate career path open to him. The hourly worker need not excuse his failure to become a department chief. All understand that the opportunity really does not exist. On the other hand, sheer tenure and mediocrity will virtually assure the executive class of reaching a rather exclusive level in much the way that a second lieutenant is assured the rank of colonel if he keeps his nose clean and is loyal to the values of the organization. As Dubin says, "Promotions within a career pattern are neither freely withheld nor freely granted by management."[9] Marked ability may speed up a career or take an individual to the levels the merely competent do not normally reach. But high office is probably no better indication of great capacity than low office is of mean abilities. To believe that all the Rickovers become admirals despite the obvious distaste of important power groups is naive. No group with the power to promote seeks sheer ability. The fact would not be worth stating if the claim of superior ability were not so continually trumpeted by those in positions of corporate power. One finds it a little difficult to sympathize with the business executives who speak of the current shortage of executive talent. In the light of widespread nepotism and favoritism shown to close friends, it often sounds as though they were complaining about a lack of relatives and buddies. Much time could be spent demonstrating that business executives are not selected wholly on their ability to increase corporate profits, but instead the relative weighing of a host of factors seems adequately summed up in the selection of Wendell Willkie as president of Commonwealth and Southern. This man of marked ability was offered the job on three

[9]Robert Dubin, *The World of Work*, Englewood Cliffs, N. J., Prentice-Hall, 1958, p. 282.

conditions: that he stop biting his fingernails, that he get his suits pressed more often, and that he have the gold in his front teeth replaced by porcelain. One is forced to wonder what the board would have done had he rejected these conditions.

It is unfortunate that the social content of economic decisions seems clearest in those instances where it is contradictory to economic considerations, since this apparently suggests that the social character of the organization is incompatible with high levels of efficiency. Nothing could, of course, be further from the truth. The relative efficiency with which American industry produces and distributes the goods and services we enjoy is impressive. And to deny this is patently ridiculous. On the other hand, it is manifest that business organizations are still immature and tolerate inefficiencies where waste is least tolerable: the provision of materials for living. In part, the problem of assessing corporate performance is dominated by the widespread belief that profit maximization is the proper corporate goal, when "there is evidence that the psychology of corporation executives has little to do with maximization of corporate profits as things now stand."[10]

What is needed is some concept of efficiency more accurate than profit maximization. Some suggest the concept of long-run profit maximization, which is almost completely devoid of meaning as a standard for judging performance. New criteria are being developed; even stockholders are concerned with the welfare of labor, perhaps recognizing that organizational vigor requires more than minimal cooperativeness from all employees. But the theory of organizations is not yet capable of more than suggesting some of the measures of corporate efficiency. While it is clear that the greatest efficiency cannot be achieved by an iron hand of wages that practices a brutal thrift in its payment for labor, there is ample evidence that nonhuman resource costs, such as those of power or raw materials, can be justifiably minimized.

The following two chapters are concerned with the way in which businesses deal with specific problems where minimizing costs or maximizing returns are reasonably satisfactory criteria for the judging of corporate behavior. The evidence seems to indicate that the social influence of culture, class, or group permeate even those areas where a hard-headed approach to efficiency or profit maximization poses no organizational threat.

[10]Allen M. Sievers, *Revolution, Evolution and the Economic Order*, Englewood Cliffs, N. J., Prentice-Hall, 1962, p. 92.

8 ▶

The Advertising Appropriation:
An Organizational Decision

Business decisions are all economic decisions. That is, business decisions always have economic consequences and are supposedly made on the basis of those consequences. Since economic behavior is instrumental and requires the prediction of results, it makes considerable sense to think of various classes of business decisions in terms of the relative certainty with which their consequences can be predicted. The simplest decisions concern the purchase of identical or easily comparable items when prices differ. The full economic consequences of buying a particular grade of wheat at $1.90 a bushel rather than at $2.05 a bushel is readily apparent to the milling company. When middle-eastern crude is $1.00 a barrel and U. S. crude is $2.95, the petroleum company will buy as much as possible of the lower priced supply despite certain qualitative differences. Other decisions, such as that to conduct research into the nature of interferons, may represent the extreme in economic uncertainity. The research might lead to a cure for cancer or other viral diseases or to nothing of commercial value.

There is no problem in determining what criteria a firm uses in purchasing middle-eastern petroleum rather than U. S. crude; they are economic criteria. It is very difficult to determine what criteria a pharmaceutical company will use in determining whether to expend money on interferon research, but they can hardly be realistically economic even with the use of the most recent decision-making techniques. The continual thesis of this volume is that where economic consequences are not clear, other considerations will always intrude upon — and may dominate — the decision-making process.

This chapter will attempt to show how the noneconomic considerations intrude, become ritualized, and even resist the application

114

of economic criteria when later developments make it possible to use them. For this purpose decisions concerning the advertising budget will be used, since the relationship between the amount spent on advertising and the effects of what advertising is understood about as well (or about as poorly) as cause-and-effect relationships in a broad range of managerial problems, such as hiring and promoting managerial personnel or determining product characteristics. Also, a study I conducted a few years ago gives me greater confidence in my understanding of the niceties of the problem that I have in most areas of business decision-making.[1]

A Rational Approach to the Advertising Budget

For most products or services there is such a thing as too much advertising and such a thing as too little advertising. The firm that advertises too little is one that has a product many people would want if they knew of the product and what it would do for them. Additional advertising would increase sales, and the profit from these sales would more than offset the advertising cost. This would probably be the situation if a roadside restaurant failed to have even a sign indicating that it sold food. Perhaps for as little as $50 it could purchase a sign that would increase its profits by $40 a week, since many more people would see that it was a restaurant and stop. But the total amount of money the restaurant could economically put into advertising would probably be small. If it placed more signs up and down the highway for several miles so that there was a total of thirty-five signs, each costing $50, it could hardly expect to have its profits grow by $40 a week for each of these signs, although they might grow by more in any time period than the signs cost during that time period. But at some point, the number of signs would be so large that no single additional sign would attract another customer or deliver another penny of profit. Obviously, the economic decision would be to build the number of signs that would return the highest profit, whether this be one or seven or thirty or several hundred.[2]

---

[1]This chapter is based largely on W. T. Tucker, *Advertising Appropriations Methods in Banking*, Atlanta, Georgia State College Bureau of Business and Economic Research, 1959.

[2]Students of economics will recognize that this chapter is generally concerned with the question of whether firms use marginal analysis in allocating funds to advertising.

The question of how much money should be spent on signs or all advertising is related to the kind of advertising that is done, the way in which the product is changed from time to time, and a host of other factors. These other factors that influence the effectiveness of advertising make it quite difficult to predict results except in a rather general way. In an industry that is characterized by continual product innovation, it may be virtually impossible to predict what any given amount of advertising will accomplish, largely because one cannot predict what competitors may do. But in a more settled business, such as banking, one would imagine that some rather shrewd deductions could be made. This is not to suggest that predicting the results of bank advertising would be easy. A large number of relevant factors, such as the number of people in the community and their relative incomes, change continually. Some other factors change less often, such as interest rates, bank services, and the number of branches (where branch banking is permitted). Still, it seems likely that anyone interested in expending the most profitable amount for bank advertising would analyze the problem in roughly the following way.

First, he would attempt to estimate how much a new account or new loan was worth in terms of profit. While this may be a somewhat difficult task and one that does not permit great precision, it should not be difficult to estimate the size and longevity of accounts, the use of funds, and therefore the profitability of accounts. In practice this might be fairly complex (much more difficult than estimating the profit on a can of beans), but still possible for a reasonably trained analyst such as an accountant or statistician to accomplish in a fairly brief period. This would give the manager a bench mark for the greatest amount of advertising that could be spent for a single bank account or loan.

Second, the manager would attempt to allocate his advertising according to its purpose. That is, he would attempt to determine how much should be considered a cost of getting loans, how much a cost of getting savings accounts, how much a cost of getting checking accounts, and the like. Of course, since some of the advertising would be quite general, certain arbitrary decisions that are routine in cost accounting would have to be made in allocating certain percentages of the cost of institutional advertising to the various services.

Lastly, the manager would want a record of the number of new users of each of the various services of the bank at least yearly, and perhaps quarterly. With these three pieces of information, the manager could determine the relationship of the average advertising cost per unit to average profitability. Of course, this would not solve all his problems in attempting to behave rationally, but it would give him a considerable start. Combined with the knowledge that more advertising will bring in more business and that the cost of bringing in more business will vary depending on whether his costs are increasing or decreasing, it would almost automatically suggest something about rational behavior for the subsequent year.[3]

For example, imagine that you are the advertising manager of a bank and that you discover that your current advertising expenditures per loan are $.21 and per new account $.80. Further, imagine that you have already determined that an average account has a profit value of $60.00. The temptation would be strong to increase the savings and checking account advertising slightly on the assumption that even if you could not get further accounts for $.80 per account in additional advertising, you might be able to get them for $3.00 or $5.00 or $12.00 in advertising with a considerable profit. If, on the other hand, you found that the average advertising cost per new account was $36.00, you might well try reducing your advertising for new accounts on the presumption that you may already be overadvertising that service. The assumption here is that if the average cost per account were $36.00, the cost of acquiring the last account was probably a good deal larger than that amount, and quite possibly greater than the $60.00 profit available over the life of the account.

An experience over several years with changing allocations for advertising would probably make it possible to make continually better estimates of whether the amount of advertising for any single service should be increased or decreased, despite other sources of variability. While these efforts would not lead to perfect profit maximization, they might lead to a reasonable approximation of that ideal, and they would at least point to the strong interest the organization had in increasing its profits or behaving rationally in the usual economic sense of that term. There is considerable evidence that in 1959 no bank in the United States was comparing its advertising cost per new account with the profitability of new accounts. *Most bank advertising managers probably never calculated their advertising expenditures in terms of any moderately direct result.*

[3]See W. T. Tucker, *op. cit.*, for evidence that bank advertising is effective and that it is generally an increasing cost proposition.

Formal Appropriations Methods

How did bank advertising managers go about setting their advertising appropriations? The four principal methods said to be used are very similar to the four methods common to advertisers in general They are:

Arbitrary: a sum established according to the policy maker's estimate of what would be proper, not supported by evidence or data.

Percentage of Deposits: from $300 to $1,000 per million of deposits, depending upon the size of the bank. This roughly equates with the percentage-of-sales method used in other businesses.

Competitive Parity: an approximation of what competitors spend, with relative size a factor.

Research-Objective or Task-Oriented: appropriation based on a set of proposed activities that have a definite purpose or goal.

The first three of these methods are under continual fire in banking simply because they do not even pretend to satisfy the profit-maximization dictum. The arbitrary method has not even the advantage of a rationale, since decisions are based only on what someone wants to spend on advertising. Despite this obvious shortcoming, some banks admit to its use. The percentage-of-deposits method ties the advertising allocation to bank size, which is clearly inappropriate. The method could readily result in relatively heavy expenditures by a bank that had already reached most of its potential market and would tend to prevent growth in the small bank with a large number of potential customers who were unaware of its existence or its range of services.

Since it may be common to assume that "everybody knows about banks," perhaps it is worth pointing out that in numerous market surveys, rather woeful ignorance on the part of large segments of the community has been demonstrated. A small bank in Florida discovered that fewer than 26 percent of the people living within two miles of its building even knew the bank existed. A subsequent advertising campaign led to rapid growth. Most people are not really aware of the difference between savings-and-loan associations and commercial banks. A fairly large number of persons with savings accounts apparently do not know how much interest they are receiving. And as incomes rise, large numbers of persons who are not knowledgeable about bank services become prospects for them.

Both the American Bankers Association and the Financial Public Relations Association publish information on the average advertising expenditures of banks by size groups in terms of a percentage of deposits. While neither association recommends the use of deposits as a criterion for the advertising appropriation, both suggest that a bank may want to see what others of its size are doing and should probably assess its own behavior carefully if it is seriously out of line with average practice. In general, it is probably true that large banks have more opportunity to increase their business through the use of advertising than small banks. Relating advertising expenditures to size has, therefore, some justification. In addition, the retention of business may require some advertising. But each bank is, finally, a special case and probably cannot even approximately maximize its profits simply by relating advertising expenditures to deposits — especially since no one is at all sure what percentage of deposits is the most effective.

The competitive-parity method has obvious difficulties in application. If two banks of the same size and in the same town spend different amounts on advertising, which one should conform to the other? Or if one bank is really maximizing its return, why should it seek competitive parity with a nearby bank that is not? Ultimately the competitive-parity concept delivers the decisions of the organization into the hands of its competitors in a slavish fashion that could only by sheerest chance result in the most profitable allocation of resources to advertising.

The fourth method receives considerable support as the most rational. Support for this point of view can be found throughout the literature on advertising.[4] The method consists of selecting a goal for advertising during the year. Most students of the problem stress the need for a specific goal rather than a vague one. Given this goal, the advertising manager is to plan his campaign to achieve the desired results. This means that he determines the media to be used and the frequency of use and calculates the costs of this specific program. In theory this kind of approach to the problem is vastly superior to merely designating a sum of money for the advertising manager to divide up in the best way he can.

The appeal of the method is obvious, since it is analogous to the sequence of events normally followed in planning a civil engineering

[4]See Albert Wesley Frey, *How Many Dollars for Advertising?*, New York, Ronald, 1955, or almost any recent text in advertising.

project. But there is little evidence that an advertising manager is dealing with anything as measurable as construction materials. There is literally no way of determining just how many people will hear a radio spot announcement that is repeated 49 times a week for 13 weeks. Nor is there any satisfactory method of predicting the response of those who do hear it.

Further, there is no assurance that the objective selected is itself economically feasible, even if the advertising manager can determine the program that would achieve it. In short, none of the methods discussed in the literature is even moderately rigorous in its pursuit of profit maximization.

One becomes even more confused on examining methods in use. The so-called allocation techniques are in practice strangely unlike their book descriptions. The following conversations are typical of ones I have had in discussions with bank advertising managers.

> *Manager A:* We use the research objective method. We start out by deciding what we want to accomplish during the year. Then I figure out the size of ads and how often we ought to run them, how many radio commercials, that kind of thing. Then we figure out what it will cost, adding in production and all of that.

> *Question:* How much did that come to last year?

> *A:* Well, our budget was a little high last year. Up about 15 percent from the year before. We expect to trim it back a little this year.

> *Q:* And how much was it?

> *A:* (Long pause) About $————.

> *Q:* And what would you say that your major objective was last year?

> *A:* Well, we wanted to increase business, of course. Savings. That was one of our big objectives.

> *Q:* About how many new savings accounts did you get?

> *A:* I could find out by calling the cashier. It would take just a minute. But you know figures like that don't really tell anything. A lot of people come in because the bank is convenient. You can't really relate new accounts to advertising.

> *Manager B:* For one thing, we always look at those FPRA statistics. We want to see what other banks our size are doing. I figure out a percent of deposits from that.

Q: And what percent do you use?

A: I think it's about a thousand dollars on the million. Something like that.

Q: I thought banks in your size group averaged about five hundred on the million.

A: Well, of course, we take into consideration the fact that this is a mighty aggressive town for bank advertising. Our president is a little different from most presidents, you know. He says if you are going to get them to come all the way up here from the south end of town, you have to tell them what you are going to do for them. We want to make sure that every last person in town knows where we are and what services we offer. (The appropriation turns out to be about $1,500 on the million.)

From dozens of conversations like this with dozens of bankers and bank advertising managers, one reaches the inevitable conclusion that advertising allocations are not generally made in any of the ways suggested in the literature. Or, more accurately, one gathers that all four of the methods suggested form only a partial list of the considerations taken into account when any bank makes out its annual budget. And the conclusion is that a change in methods will not change the amount appropriated by a given bank more than slightly, unless either the circumstances or people involved are changed also. That is, the actual method used is simply bargaining among executives, with certain features of the context having a relatively high degree of salience. Listing the critical features of this bargaining process is not completely satisfactory, since it tends to disregard the dynamic character of the situation. In all probability the best account of the process would take into account the power structure of the executive group, its characteristic methods of search, the groups involved in the process, their particular aims and values, and a number of procedural or behavioral operations. Since the resulting analysis would be merely a particularized discussion of social interaction, the actual turning points would undoubtedly seem unique and suggest that the process could only be understood in terms of place, time, the actual individuals involved, and so forth.

Factors that Influence Appropriations

One can sensibly think of the process of allocating advertising appropriations as being largely related to the interaction of several factors. Primary among these factors are the president, the past, the profits, and the competition. Since each of these terms is intended to designate a rather complex notion, further definition is required.

The President. The character of the small bank may be established largely by its president, the character of the larger bank by the interaction of a number of executives. This character may realistically be spoken of as aggressive or conservative, public spirited or selfish. And advertising is likely to be one of the more visible symptoms of that character. Most banks today are relatively eager to make small, consumer loans. Yet even a few years ago a reasonably large number did not seek these out — even refused to grant them (except perhaps to certain honored customers). Others were frankly not interested in small savings or checking accounts. Either the dignity or the conservatism of the bank made finance-company tactics seem undesirable. Quite obviously such banks could not mount the kind of advertising campaign characteristic of the go-getters who had been, over the past twenty years, changing traditional banking methods. Some bankers still resist anything but the blandest institutional advertising, such as "good" music programs and newspaper advertisements that talk vaguely about citizenship or the importance of credit in economic growth. The kind of advertising done influences the amount of money spent on advertising. And the character of the bank determines the kind of advertising. In part the reason for suggesting that the bank character is related to the president is that the most spectacular changes in bank character (and the amount of advertising done) have attended changes in the presidency. In the case of a small Southern bank, for example, a new president increased the advertising budget by 500 percent. But this was merely symptomatic of a change in the entire character of the bank. It was renovated both inside and out to look less like the traditional bank, new services were added, and several personnel and organizational changes were made.

The Past. Advertising appropriations are always thought of in terms of last year's appropriation. In the executive bargaining that establishes the budget, last year is a constant point of reference, and the years before may well be referred to. The question before the committee is not "How much shall we spend for advertising?" but "How much more or less than last year shall we spend?" In any discussion of advertising appropriations, the reference to percentage increases and decreases is constant. For example, one advertising

manager pointed out that the appropriation was not as large as he
or the president would like to see it, but that it had been increased
by about twenty percent each of the previous two years, which was
"a larger budgetary increase than any other department received."

The Profits.   It is a truism in business that decreased profits
normally lead to tighter budgets and increased profits to looser ones.
This is exactly the reverse of the economic concept that expenditures
are made to influence profits. Profit itself is not, of course, as important an influence as the availability of resources. An extremely strong
company may increase advertising in the face of decreasing profits
in an attempt to attract more business. The financially weaker organization is less likely to take such a risk. Bank advertising managers indicate that they are sensitive to profits in their budgetary
requests, making their greatest demands for increases at the end of
profitable years and merely trying to maintain their position or get
slight increases in what they consider less favorable circumstances.
Of course, profits in banking do not fluctuate as wildly as they do in
many industries. The year of great loss in some businesses may be
the spur to model changes and aggressive promotion, although such
reactions are apparently "modern" and not universally approved.
In banking, where the security of account holders' funds is the paramount consideration, such bold reactions to financial reverses are
unlikely — as are serious financial reverses themselves.

It should be pointed out that a bank probably shows little immediate profit on the acquisition of most new accounts and that
profitability in any given year could probably be improved by limiting
expenditures to the small amount of loan advertising that would
maintain a near loaned-out position. The fact that few banks accept
such a course is undoubtedly related to the institutional values.
Banks, like insurance companies, are highly cognizant of the long run
and are tempted to think of themselves as permanent organizations.
This would suggest that, more than other firms, they would tend not
to behave in a profit-maximizing way, since the profit maximization
of economic theory is a relatively short-term concept.

The Competition.   Banks in any given locality tend to conform
to local standards. Where one bank disengages itself from the non-
competitive understandings of the clearing house, others soon follow.
Bank competition in Miami is stronger than that in Columbus, Ohio,
and the most conservative banks in the former city have relatively
larger advertising budgets than the least conservative in the latter.

The activities of finance companies and savings-and-loan associations must also influence the climate within which decisions are made. In fact, the entire current emphasis on heavy consumer advertising and a maximum of amortized small loans is undoubtedly a reaction to the postwar successes of the finance company. Any Atlanta banker can attest to his own changes in behavior (including increased advertising appropriations) after Mills B. Lane became president of the Citizens and Southern Bank.

Certainly it is dangerous to reach any conclusions about all business decisions from the study of advertising-appropriations methods in banking. But the suggestion is clear that economic theory is a bit too cool, precise, and thin to encompass the business decision, which must deal with many considerations other than short-term profits. The mere fact that banks have not learned how to relate advertising appropriations to profits in any rigorous fashion when it would not be particularly difficult to make progress in that direction suggests that bankers view their task as richer, more varied, and less specific than does economic theory.

If there is room for complaint it would seem to be that the banker (or perhaps all businessmen) has been so thoroughly sold on the economic concept that he attempts to explain virtually all his activities in economic terms. And, in so doing he often gulls himself, becoming less aware of his own motives and decision-making processes than he should be. The false rationale of the task-oriented advertising budget may be a useful social tool with which to keep others from complaining about the way in which one carries out a difficult task. Its danger lies in the strong possibility that the one who uses it may come to believe that he is actually trying to maximize profits and that this is a method by which those maximum profits can be achieved.

9 ▶

International Business

While all economic decisions are influenced by social consid-erations, those that include participants from different cultures often hinge on completely unexpected factors. Often neither party is able to anticipate the other's behavior with any degree of certainty or understand it in retrospect. Only occasionally does one encounter within his own nation the kind of upsetting uncertainty that plagues international business.

True, the plumber in the Smoky Mountains of North Carolina may not show up on the job because the weather is too good. (When it is perfect hunting or fishing weather, job contracts may be called off unilaterally by either party without any sense of delinquency.) But most of the time it is possible to determine with considerable accuracy what others feel and approximately how they will behave. This is simply not so in international situations.

Cultural Barriers to Trade

Such small matters as promptness are cultural as well as personal. A nine o'clock appointment does not mean the same thing in Singa-pore, Ankara, London, and Santiago. The nature of appropriate physical contact varies as well. The American businessman may shrink from the enthusiastic hugs of a Columbian in the same way a native of Calcutta shrinks from an American handshake. Of course, these are well-known and minor considerations, but they suggest something of the height of the cultural barrier that hampers inter-national trade, even when it is economically advantageous.

The simplest solution to the problem of international trade is simply to avoid it, although this may be a highly uneconomic solution.

But prejudice against foreigners or things foreign, ethnocentrism, is a common social response of many groups of people in all lands. E. M. Forester's *A Passage to India* suggests that it cannot be completely overcome even by those with considerable goodwill. The result is that savings accounts do not flood into Latin America from the United States, although the interest paid on them may be two or even three times as great as can be realized locally and security is comparable to domestic investment. The furniture retailer may refuse to consider the purchase of foreign furniture either because of misguided "patriotism" or the ridiculous notion that "all foreign products are poorly made." And the chamber of commerce secretary who would really like to purchase a Volkswagen buys an American car instead as a demonstration of loyalty. Very clearly, the mutual suspicion and distrust that characterize intercultural exchange serve to limit economic activities that cross national borders. As Robinson says:

> My research has indicated that many, if not most, American managements summarily reject all foreign opportunities without regard for the business lost by inaction. Such a closed mind, I found, generally precluded any serious investigation, any careful weighing of overseas business opportunities, any analysis of foreign markets. In such cases, how does the businessman know he is getting the highest return on this investment?[1]

The strength of ethnocentric public opinion even precludes, through governmental activities, certain kinds of economically advantageous activities. While one could spend considerable time discussing the economic folly of many tariffs, quotas, and other trade restrictions, it is obvious that free world trade is no economic panacea at the present time. The construction of the European Common Market entailed more than the overcoming of excessive nationalism and mutual suspicion. Real economic dangers existed in the joining of diverse economies, and these had to be guarded against with considerable care. Yet there is little question in anyone's mind that the major deterrent to the union was such strong national antipathies as those between France and Germany.

Much clearer examples of noneconomic behavior exist in many of the restrictions of foreign investments. It is quite common for

[1]Richard D. Robinson, *Cases in International Business*, New York, Holt, 1962, p. 2.

nations to write laws prohibiting foreign control of certain kinds of industries, especially communications or extractive industries, despite the need for developmental funds. Expropriation is not uncommon, even when this clearly restricts the possibility of attracting additional foreign capital and in some cases decreases the economic return to the expropriating nation. Other restrictions on currency exchange or the use of imported labor may completely prevent some operations that would be of economic value. National pride is such that it is not uncommon for underdeveloped nations to encourage "showy" developments, such as hydroelectric facilities, steel plants, and railroads, even when these cannot be expected to yield as good a return on investment as other developmental strategies. We in the United States on occasion behave as uneconomically as any underdeveloped nation. The British have long complained about the United States government's encouraging bids on such major equipment as generators, only to refuse the low bid when it is British.[2]

Yet despite the hedgehog of legal considerations discouraging international business, there is wide latitude for successful actions of private enterprise. But in these it is a commonplace that purely economic considerations are not the *sine qua non* of successful business. Almost every observer of the resurgence of German trade in Latin America gives major credit to social factors. The Germans come to stay; they make friends with the nationals; they learn the language; they frequently become citizens, marry natives, or send their children to local schools. Behavior of this sort is undoubtedly as important as adapting products for Latin American usage, an advantageous price structure, and good quality control in the success of many German firms and products.

In general, international business is carried on by exporting, by licensing a foreign manufacturer to produce certain items, or by establishing manufacturing facilities in a foreign country. Quite obviously, the degree of involvement between cultures varies from the limited contacts required for the sale of industrial goods between businessmen (who have many subcultural similarities) to the extensive and continuous relationships that attend the organization of both productive and distributional facilities.

[2]Of course, all decisions of the sort examined in this paragraph are not necessarily uneconomic. Frequently there is some short-term or long-term advantage to which proponents can refer without obvious sophistry.

Adapting to Foreign Markets

The most readily anticipated problem is that of adapting products for a different culture. But, even here it is remarkably easy to assume cultural similarities that do not exist. According to A. S. Hart:

> We started by taking a product we made here — like Quaker Oats — and trying to convince people overseas to use that item the way we did. Two things happened: they wouldn't use the product at all, or they wouldn't use it in the same way. In the second case we were at least partially successful; in the first, we had to change the item altogether.
>
> But, gradually we came to realize that we were not in the oatmeal field at all — we were in the food business. What do you do when you are in the food business? You make things people want to eat. So, we have designed products to fit the particular markets where we operate. Some of the items we have developed are not made in the United States at all, and wouldn't be suited to the tastes of our customers here.[3]

Similar product changes are common in nonfood items. Radios, vacuum cleaners, refrigerators, and automobiles are normally modified for export. The Volkswagens, Renaults, and Volvos sold in this country are export models differing from the same makes sold at home. Ford's Cardinal, at one time considered for sale in the United States, is available only in foreign markets. During the late forties, Chrysler sold an export Dodge that was in reality a Plymouth with certain modifications such as the Dodge grill, since light weight and low gas consumption are highly favored in Europe — along with names suggesting cars above the "economy" class.

Just as products must be adapted for local use, so must the means by which they are sold. Advertising, which has been largely an American development, opens the way to numerous cross-cultural blunders. Even such a knowledgeable international operator as Coca-Cola occasionally makes mistakes, as it did in the advertisement in Italy showing Mario Lanza dressed as Enrico Caruso. Italian opera-lovers (and apparently this includes virtually the entire adult population) were up in arms at what was interpreted as a commercial slur on a national hero. Mistakes of this sort do not necessarily mean that international promotion should make use of foreign advertising agencies any more than that companies should use other foreign

[3]Dan H. Fenn, Jr., *Management Guide to Overseas Operations*, New York, McGraw-Hill, 1957, p. 197.

techniques. While foreign advertising agencies may be accutely aware of the cultural values in a particular locality, they are often less able to utilize those "American" techniques that are effective abroad. In consequence, most of the large agencies and international operations have had to develop foreign offices and train personnel who understand both American methods and local customs and values.

Even the simplest of foreign operation requires the personal interactions of individuals with diverse backgrounds. At least a foreign distributor, purchaser, or representative must be personally dealt with by the exporting organization. "It is well known," according to Herskovits, "that where a non-European has to deal with a European in a matter involving trade, both parties to the transaction are subject to no little irritation because of different traditions of trading."[4] Not only can irritation between persons of culturally different backgrounds prevent the development of a useful economic relationship, but also — perhaps more important — the cultural differences themselves may prevent either party from understanding the kind of individual he is dealing with. Judgment of individuals is always difficult, yet necessary to successful commercial relationships. It can be virtually impossible to judge the diligence, intelligence, sincerity, or sympathy of someone from an unfamiliar culture. For instance, in many cultures the offering or acceptance of bribes is no indication of dishonesty, and verbal agreement may be a form of politeness that does not even indicate understanding.

Further, since business methods are more clearly cultural than rational, even the selection of the most satisfactory foreign associates may signal the beginning of a sequence of awkward mutual accommodations. Traditionally, most foreign businessmen have thought in terms of limited markets and high profit per unit. While the postwar trend toward heavy promotion and low unit profit as a way toward maximum sales and good profitability has been strong (with firms like Olivetti demonstrating greater ability to utilize "American" techniques than many American firms), the older tradition still exists in most areas. This means that the foreign distributor of American goods will often be out of sympathy with the manufacturer's promotional methods and disinclined to use them in his territory. It may take years to encourage such a distributor to become an organizational member who follows home-office policies with vigor.

[4]Melville J. Herskovits, *Economic Anthropology*, New York, Knopf, 1952, p. 37.

Overseas Production

It is increasingly difficult for a company of any size to carry out international activities on the basis of a limited number of foreign distributors. Foreign exchange problems, the strong interest in economic development in all parts of the world, and labor cost differentials often force the firm that wants more world business to manufacture abroad. While occasional meetings between businessmen of different cultural backgrounds can be perplexing, the development of an organization in which the cultures rub against one another daily, as they do in a foreign plant, is far more difficult. The problems involved are, of course, seldom economic and demonstrate the extent to which apparently economic considerations in our own culture are in reality cultural. As Herskovits points out: ". . . while every culture must operate efficiently enough to ensure that its human carriers survive, it does not follow that this efficiency is as apparent when viewed from outside the culture as it appears to those who carry out the traditions under which it is sanctioned.[5]

Most foreign installations, either because of legal requirements or because of economic wisdom, are at least partly owned by nationals and largely staffed by nationals. Typically, this means that the two cultures come together at several organizational levels. In the process, not only their cultures but their legitimate economic interests will clash from time to time.

Workers in many lands, perhaps most, are more widely separated from managerial and ownership groups than they are in the United States. In part, this may be related to the fact that in many parts of the world owners have traditionally been somewhat more oppressive than in the United States. (Of course, both these characteristics may be strongly related to the level of economic development. Laboring men have never fared well during the early stages of industrialization — often living under worse conditions than their more primitive ancestors.)

Workers are often, therefore, not in sympathy with capitalism. Many of them see socialism as the only real cure for their own economic problems (although it is a mistake to regard their economic or political philosophies as sophisticated) and might be compared with the more radical work groups in this nation in the late nineteenth century. American managers may mistakenly believe these attitudes

[5]Herskovits, *op. cit.*, p. 80.

to be simple-minded misunderstandings of economic reality, even when they are, in fact, expressions of class conflict. Real hatred for owners and managers is not unusual, although it is probably most often hatred for a class rather than for individuals. Sincere and ardent communists are extremely likely to make up a part of the work force. The tensions that exist are much like those of a feudal system in which the peasant regards himself as exploited by the baron yet can see no way to satisfy his own immediate economic needs save by working for him until some vaguely perceived day of reckoning.

As would be expected under rigid class systems, superficial forms of politeness and subservience are likely to be emphasized. The worker goes to some length to tell the boss what he thinks the boss wants to hear, even if the truth is severely bent in the process. Frankness is seldom characteristic of a class-bound society. Obviously, the worker is unlikely to admit that he does not understand a particular job when asked. He is willing under slight encouragement to promise a speed of performance that is completely imaginary. And when he fails to live up to his promises, he is likely to regard being held to them an extreme injustice. In the underdeveloped nations of the world, and especially those where illiteracy rates are high, story telling reaches the fanciful heights of the American frontier. The native worker may be talking Paul Bunyan or Sal Fink or Davy Crockett when the manager thinks he is talking business. Unfortunately, the highest flights of fancy are often regarded with awe and are generally delivered with a straight face. But the story-teller does not expect the tall tale to be believed; it is designed to call forth admiration. After all, the manager is supposed to know the truth of the matter, whatever it is, far better than the worker.

Escape from blame can be a far more serious demand in many areas than it is in the United States, where it is given great indulgence, especially in executive circles. Alibi Ike is not a peculiarly American character, although he may be understood and recognized best in his own milieu. And as one learns not to listen when a Democratic President blames all the nation's ills on the Republican members of Congress, the American businessman abroad must learn to ignore a number of the fanciful excuses and explanations of the native employee.

Lastly, the employee is liable to demand personal attention that an American worker would find objectionable. The plant manager may be asked to arrange the marriage of two workers as though he were chief of the tribe or patriarch of the great family. Workers may rely on him for personal loans or medical care or advice in personal matters. Kemal Seli, an Americanized Turk who returned to his native land to set up a rug factory, found it necessary to protect his female workers on their way home from the plant — even going to the lengths of capturing two molesters personally.[6]

While generalizations such as these can be made, differences from culture to culture and those between individuals within a single culture can be great. According to Virginia Thompson, the Chinese, Indians, and Malayans in Malaya have quite different preferences (or tolerances) in work. The Chinese, for example, typically prefer piece-rates since this allows them to get a greater return for diligence.[7] The Malayans, on the other hand, demonstrate little interest in money beyond that which will provide for their immediate subsistence. The traditions of Japan require that in calculating wages the firm use a large number of components "typically including a minimum rate, a basic rate, family allowance, seasonal bonus, overtime payment, cost-of-living adjustment, regional allowance, transportation and housing allowance, skill and job-status premium, extra pay for hazardous and dirty work, and the like."[8] The list says much about the high degree of social involvement between firm and worker, especially when compared with the relative independence of the Chinese in Southeast Asia who prefer piece-rates.

But generalizations at this level are inherently dangerous because they encourage the businessman to think in terms of the typical Mexican, Indonesian, or Turk. Individual differences are great in all parts of the world and become critical in the establishment of a new industry with its demands for the development of a whole list of new skills and new social relationships within the firm. The character of the informal organization, necessary to the operation of any business, will depend on the location of atypical Indians, just as it does on the location of atypical Americans in domestic industry.

Paternalism is clearly the rule in most foreign operations. But it is not merely a paternalism imposed by entrepreneurs; it is a paternalism demanded by the workers. Further, the appropriate degree of paternalism varies from place to place and over time. In some

[6]Robinson, *op. cit.*, p. 128.
[7]Virginia Thompson, *Labor Problems in Southeast Asia*, New Haven, Yale University Press, 1947, p. 77.
[8]Solomon B. Levine, *Industrial Relations in Postwar Japan*, Urbana, Ill., University of Illinois Press, 1958, p. 116.

cases it encourages the economic anomaly of labor unions with officers who are also officers of the company, as in prewar Japan. In others the symptoms of paternalistic social relations are seen in the seeking out of lawyers and politicians as union members and leaders, although management is excluded. According to Fayerweather, those who are new to international business tend to underestimate the paternalistic requirements, while many who have long experience in foreign projects fail to see the rapidity with which workers in their operations are becoming eager for greater responsibility and independence.[9]

Obviously, in some localities the rate of pay offered workers may be considerably less important in establishing an effective labor force than a willingness on the part of executives to manage numerous aspects of the workers' lives. It has been demonstrated in many cases that wages can be too high. That is, where wages outrun the worker's day-to-day needs by a wide margin, he may simply quit working after a short time or absent himself with considerable frequency. U. S. Steel in its first Mexican operation found it necessary to teach workers the advantage of higher levels of consumption in order to keep their relatively high wages from disrupting the work force.

First-line supervisory techniques are apt to vary greatly from those of a San Diego or Rochester plant. Since most nations insist on a labor force that is about 85 percent native and since the language abilities of American supervisors do not encourage foreign assignments, native foremen and crew bosses are common. Training such people in the technical aspects of their jobs is often the smaller part of the managerial problem (and is quite frequently solved by requiring less decision-making than is typical of foremen in American industry). Petty tyranny and physical violence are apt to occur as the traditional ways of overcoming worker ineptitude and resistance to direction. Labor itself may virtually insist on such treatment at the same time that it reacts angrily to it. Most enlightened management cannot tolerate crew-boss methods that so clearly state the existence of extreme class difference as well as virtual enmity between labor and management. Yet it may be forced to tolerate such activities in order to get work done. Under such circumstances it is difficult for the American manager to view immediate productivity as his single goal.

[9]John Fayerweather, *Management of International Operations*, New York, McGraw-Hill, 1960, pp. 283–284.

Almost universally he feels it necessary to work toward the standards of personal relationships that he is sure are "right" in business and industry. And his standards of "right" are normally the impersonal accommodations typical in the United States. In effect, he tears at the social fabric he finds, lowering the status of the native supervisors or managers by requiring that they act more like the equals of those they direct than they, themselves, regard as appropriate.

The Businessman as a Cultural Missionary

It is clear that the American firm and its managers are social reformers. They do not like the appurtenances of class that they find abroad, and they attempt to modify them, at least within the confines of their own operation. Upper-class Latin American youths are encouraged to train for management positions by starting out in menial occupations that they cannot accept. The American company will not insist, but it will continue to push, attempting to locate one here or one there who will accede to its wishes. And it will undoubtedly value such persons highly, probably rewarding them above their less "Americanized" fellows of equal ability.

Fayerweather gives the following account of the way in which a United States firm in Mexico built a U. S. form of credit union.

> A sudden change [from direct borrowing from top executives] would have been bad both because the workers were financially and morally incapable of running such an operation and because they would have resented being cut off from the executives. However, for the first few years, the credit union was run by a board including the general manager and treasurer, and applicants for loans could talk to these officers. Thus the first step of the transition did not result in a notable change in relationships, and in due course the workers acquired competence in managing the union and were weaned from dependence on the executives in at least this one respect.[10]

But it is not merely U. S. businessmen who want to establish their own types of social institutions and behavior abroad. The representatives of any economically advanced nation are dedicated to social reform. Thompson cites an example:

> Strikes have occurred and continue to occur in spite of the presence of a British Adviser sent to Burma for the purpose of fostering the growth

[10]Fayerweather, *op. cit.*, p. 284.

of trade unionism, largely because the workers' demands combine legitimate labor grievances with political objectives, which, to the British, are impossible.[11]

Efforts by Americans to establish United States-oriented credit unions and by Britains to create a British form of trade unionism are perhaps laudable. Certainly they cannot be regarded as wholly economic, or even principally economic. From the foreign worker who wants a more responsible position as a matter of pride, to the foreign businessman who finds his American counterparts too brusque and impersonal, to the American manager of the foreign enterprise who tries to teach human relations to his supervisors: all are as attentive to the social situation as they are to the economic potential of their activities.

Gunnar Myrdal goes so far as to suggest that economic theory is literally *Western* economic theory which does not apply to the situations existing in most of the world. "Economic analysis will have to deal with all of the relevant factors if it wants to be realistic," he says. "General economic theory will have to become social theory."[12] There is considerable doubt that an integration of social theory and economic theory is possible until both have been developed much further; perhaps there is not even a way in which a reasonable rapprochement between the two can be accomplished currently.

[11]Thompson, *op. cit.*, p. 54.
[12]Gunnar Myrdal, *Rich Lands and Poor*, New York, Harper, 1957, p. 102.

10 ▶

Community Economic
Development

The economic development of a community depends primarily upon natural resources, people, and tools. The proposition is so obvious that one is tempted to accept and understand it as an essentially simple-minded statement that is almost meaningless. The suggestion here is that these factors — people, natural resources, and tools — should be regarded in their social meanings if one is to understand the nature of the diverse economic decisions and activities that lead to the development of a New York City or a Southwick, Massachusetts, an El Chico, California, or a Dallas.

As Eric Zimmermann so ably pointed out, a natural resource is a resource only to those societies capable of developing it.[1] The finest natural harbor on the United States Atlantic Coast is probably that at Port Royal, South Carolina. In no meaningful sense is it a significant resource in 1963, although the nearby lesser harbors of Charleston and Savannah are. The small mines in the Black Hills of South Dakota demonstrate quite clearly the social character of resources. A typical mine of this sort has been reworked several times. The original miner pursued a vein of some wanted mineral until it gave out. Subsequent owners reworked the tailings that lay outside the shaft, collecting material that had only a few years before been waste. Many of these mines have been reworked as many as three or four times as succeeding years have seen the discovery of uses for the rare earths and minerals previously discarded as worthless.

One of the most sophisticated views of economic development

[1] Eric W. Zimmermann, *World Resources and Industries* (rev. ed.), New York, Harper, 1951, Chapters 1–3.

136

is that of C. E. Ayers.[2] While he considers tools and tool innovation to be the critical factors in growth, he sees these arising out of a combination of cultural and economic surpluses within a relevant social organization. From this point of view the full meaning of tools is generated by society's interaction with them.

The economic consequences of tools are largely dependent upon cultural change. The spinning wheel may have a certain economic value as an antique; it has none currently in the United States as a tool. The digital computer, on the other hand, has not been fully assimilated by the culture. It still has no tool uses in many companies or for many functions where its future utilization can be rather surely predicted.

Lastly, people must be regarded socially. If Clarence Birdseye, who developed the technique of freezing foods, had been in a position of some power, he might have developed the frozen food business a good five or ten years earlier. Lacking either capital or the power to command capital, he was forced to develop the industry at a snail's pace. Power should not be considered as the ownership of wealth but as the ability to bring needed resources together in a functional relationship. The apocryphal story of the Texas oilman makes the point nicely. On leaving for the East, he told his agent to bid up to $5,000,000 on the mineral rights of a particular parcel of land. He received a frantic long distance call from his agent informing him that he had succeeded in getting the rights for several hundred thousand less than his top bid but that there was a serious hitch. "What's wrong?" asked the oil man. The agent replied with some chagrin, "They want five thousand cash."

In order to discuss the problem of development in a moderately systematic fashion, this chapter will begin with the simpler and more primitive organizations, where cultural (or traditional) values frequently seem dominant, and then move toward the large, modern city with its complex power relations and its subtle class and status distinctions.

Primitive Development

It may seem gratuitous to begin with prehistoric times, but the anthropological explanation of the early development of large, func-

[2]C. E. Ayers, *The Theory of Economic Progress*, Chapel Hill, University of North Carolina Press, 1944, Chapter 6.

tional communities throws considerable light on the interrelationships of resources, tools, and people. Why should highly developed civilizations have occurred first in the Middle East rather than in Europe? Relatively rich land was plentiful in Europe. Therefore the tribal groups moved on to new land as soon as their present settlement was depleted by their agricultural activities. Land was essentially valueless, and high value was associated with things that could be moved. Personal belongings and cattle were the only consequential capital in a settlement that would be abandoned after four years or less. Partly because wealth was highly portable, theft became a way of life, with raiding parties being often the most efficient economic organization. The small, fast-moving, hard-hitting guerrilla organization was ideally suited to the situation. It was capable of warding off attack, performing raids on other groups, raising crops, herding cattle, and moving on. When the Roman legions marched north, it was to a great extent this society that they encountered.

In the Middle East, fertile land was scarce, largely limited to the bottom land of the great rivers. Periodic floods maintained fertility at reasonable levels. Undoubtedly, there must have been considerable fighting over the possession of land, but mutual agreements and joint defense arrangements probably account for the social innovation of law, which reached high levels of refinement. One may infer that animal fertilizers were used, and the elaborate ruins indicate labor specialization. Written language, a numerical system, and coinage became important tools of a social and economic system that encouraged their invention, use, and development.

There is considerable evidence that the early American farmers suffered cultural demoralization from the vast amount of fertile land available, and that as they moved west, they forgot the old world conservation of land fertility by crop rotation and animal fertilizers, so that a great deal which was in their cultural heritage had to be retaught in the twentieth century by agricultural agents of the government.

While it often seems more meaningful to talk of broad historical developments that cover generations, centuries, or millenia, the kinds of economic decisions that are made and the context within which they are made can best be seen in the individual choices made in specific situations. Further, far too little is known about the distant or even the recent past to speak of such things in any but essentially current circumstances.

The Small Community

Plainville, a small Missouri community given this pseudonym by Carl Withers (James West), provides the kind of simple, rural setting within which individual decisions can be examined with reasonable care.[3] Plainville is a rural town of some 275 families, located in an agricultural county with a population of slightly more than 5,000 persons. The economic base of the area is entirely agricultural, with small retail businesses serving the population. With two roughly distinct classes of people, the area has only a loose hierarchic organization. The potentials for social and economic progress are few and meager for the citizens of Plainville. According to West, about the only available work choices are to start farming as a small owner or tenant or to start some small retail or service business.[4] Of course, a large percentage of the young people move out of the county to nearby cities or to a section of California where former residents of the Plainville area have congregated. The emphasis on agriculture as a way to make a living can be seen in the fact that natives do not generally recognize the other opportunities of the area. More than half the business and professional men in Plainville during the mid-fifties had moved there as adults since 1939.[5] In short, the way to economic success is largely limited to agricultural activities and has been so for many years. West's study took place during the period when agricultural agents were attempting to improve farming methods and, therefore, sheds considerable light on the process of economic development. Resistance to new farming methods was great, especially to such changes as the introduction of lespedeza and the use of lime. As one farmer said, "I'd prosecute a man that puts lime on my land. Joe's place will never grow another crop."[6] Resistance to improved production methods had to be overcome gradually. The first step was invariably dependent upon the agricultural agent's ability to develop close friendships. Often his advice was taken because of this friendship rather than because of any real belief that it was of value. (One county agent in Illinois used to tell of finally

[3]The town has been one of the few that has been studied twice, as reported in James West, *Plainville, U.S.A.*, New York, Columbia University Press, 1945, and Art Gallaher, Jr., *Plainville Fifteen Years Later*, New York, Columbia University Press, 1961.
[4]West, *op. cit.*, pp. 23–24.
[5]Gallaher, *op. cit.*, p. 80.
[6]West, *op. cit.*, p. 223.

persuading a farm family with which he was on very good terms to put lime on one field. The application was made after midnight and the lime was quickly disced in so that neighbors would not know the family had taken the agent's advice.) Other farmers imitate the few who are willing to take the agent's advice, if it is successful and if the agent has chosen a relatively high-status farmer whom others are willing to imitate. So with almost every agricultural reform, even today, the county agent must find someone in the loose organization of independent farmers who will try out his ideas. And a large number of the ultimate imitators will carefully forget that the original suggestion came from the county agent. Gallaher reports that in 1954 only 10 of the 337 farms reporting dairy sales as their principal income were members of the Dairy Herd Improvement Association, in spite of the fact that it offered the only reasonably direct route to profitable herd building.[7] The reasons given for nonparticipation are many, but all seem to have a cultural base. None of this denies the tremendous growth in agricultural output during the last thirty years, but merely indicates cultural resistance to change — even changes recommended by a source that has a long record of giving profitable advice.

Other new behavioral forms seem to seize hold without economic justification because they have cultural support. Both West and Gallaher complain mildly about the farmer who purchases farm equipment that he cannot economically employ. Quite probably this is related to the farmer's traditional desire for independence — he would rather own his own equipment than rent the service from others — and his interest in acquiring the symbols of status. As West says:

> Second, some of the modern machines are nonfunctional. Tractors, for example, can be profitably used on only a few of the prairie farms, yet in 1940, as many as 145 tractors were owned by the 1,300-plus farms of the county. Some of these are found on hill farms "with no more farm land than a man and a mule could farm."[8]

In Gallaher's estimation the rate of purchasing of uneconomic farm equipment in 1954 surpassed that of fifteen years earlier. He quotes one farmer as saying:

[7]Gallaher, *op. cit.*, p. 63.
[8]West, *op. cit.*, p. 10.

"People got their own ideas — And they like to be their own boss. Soon as I git the money I'm buying me a combine. (He has about twenty-five acres of grain.) May have to git a used one like Steve Luck done, but hit'll be mine. When I git ready to combine I want hit done right now. . . don't like to depend on some feller to do hit for me. Shore, hit'll be costly, but hit'll be worth hit.[9]

Other isolated examples of activities in Plainville give some insight into the social context of economic decisions. Trading in this area, as in much of rural America, is both a social and an economic activity. West recounts a full afternoon spent over the trade for a pony and suggests that numerous participants besides the principals got their full measure of satisfaction out of the event. He goes on to quote the admiring words of one onlooker who told of that most magnificent of all trading sessions, in which a man came to town on a Saturday, traded his horse, and made nine other transactions, ending the day with his own mount and nothing but enjoyment to boot.[10]

Gallaher gives the example of a new businessman in Plainville talking with the town board and other retailers before opening a pool hall. The success of the venture depended largely on achieving a reasonable amount of public support and providing loafing place, since most of the other retailers were eliminating their traditional facilities for the older men who sat around the town square and talked all day.[11]

The most spectacular case of conflict between social and economic pressure surely was that of the game warden appointed to the county in which Plainville lay. Since local custom is to resent any outside interference and to regard game laws as unreasonable restraints on a man's natural rights, the prospective warden could find no house to rent. Those who had empty dwellings refused to do business with him. Finally, he located a house owned by a person who had moved away and who was no longer subject to the social pressures of the immediate area. But even for this he was forced to pay considerably more than the going rate, in order to salve the owner's conscience.[12]

The town that derives its income from a number of small farms is typically unorganized save by its culture and the habituation of roles. Often there is no hierarchy that can either initiate or prevent

[9]Gallaher, *op. cit.*, p. 57.
[10]West, *op. cit.*, p. 21.
[11]Gallaher, *op. cit.*, p. 77.
[12]*Ibid*, p. 149.

change, no real leadership group that can examine the local circumstances and make moves to adapt to them. Innovation in Plainville was almost entirely sent in from outside in the form of immigrating business and professional men or government employees. While no community has more than moderate control of its own destiny, a leadership or power group develops to establish policies and set goals in towns larger than Plainville. And under certain kinds of circumstances it will develop in even smaller communities. The company town, in which the social, political, and economic hierarchies are identical, can be based on large landholdings, as is Kingsville, Texas; on mining, as is Anaconda, Montana; or on manufacturing, as is Hershey, Pennsylvania. Obviously, such feudal baronies no longer exercise the absolute power they may have once enjoyed over local affairs. Many citizens of communities of this sort maintain that the power still exists but that it is manipulated in less obvious ways and is only brought to bear on issues of some importance.

Hierarchic Communities

Most American communities lie somewhere between the extremes of Plainville and of Anaconda in the organization of their power structures. The reasons for this can be traced quite easily. The Plainville that grows soon develops a number of larger economic units — banks, grain elevators, feed companies, packing plants, department stores, and the like. With face-to-face contact more difficult in the growing community and with larger powers in the hands of certain individuals, controlling classes or groups develop. On the other hand, the company town that grows almost invariably develops other concatenations of power in retailing, construction, unionization, politics, and the like. And these dilute the original power concentration. Some notion of the relative disorganization (lack of a single, controlling group) of the small city can be seen in the inability of the community leaders in Salem, Massachusetts, to agree in identifying their own most powerful members.[13] Such disorganization does not mean that there is no effective power structure so much as it means that power is not formally organized and that different segments of power are normally brought to bear on different problems.

[13]Floyd Hunter, Ruth C. Schaffer, and Cecil G. Sheps, *Community Organizations: Action and Inaction*, Chapel Hill, University of North Carolina Press, 1956, p. 35.

The power elements of the small city are no more clearly dedicated to economic progress than are the farmers of Plainville. Often they are apparently more interested in maintaining a way of life or protecting their own relative positions in the social structure. Further, there is considerable evidence that the holders of power are normally conservative, with the result that innovations important to economic development must often come from individuals intent on moving into the power positions rather than from those who are already there.

The twin cities of Champaign-Urbana exist for a single reason. The city fathers of Urbana refused to allow the Illinois Central to run its tracks through the town or to build a terminal there, reportedly because they wished to keep the town an attractive residential area. The tracks were laid, and a depot was built outside the city limits. Of course, the depot became the center of much commercial activity, and the new town of Champaign rapidly outstripped the older Urbana in size and importance. In a Southern city the results were the same, although the apparent motivation was different.

> It was not the Civil War, alone, however, that shattered Old City's past, for the coming of the railroads diminished the importance of all the river towns. Old City could have been saved if her river-minded businessmen had foreseen the advantage of letting the mainline pass through their city. After their refusal, inland towns arose on the trunk lines in Old City's former trade area to serve as outlets for seacoast distributors.[14]

Of course, it would be erroneous to create the impression that most cities fought to prevent railroads from coming through; a large number worked just as diligently to get the railroads to make their cities integral parts of the system. To insure the growing importance of its capital, the state of Indiana required that every railroad operating in the state construct a line to Indianapolis. The requirement was clearly instrumental in making Indianapolis the economic center of Indiana and the largest of its cities.

But welcoming the influx of new industry or business because of its influence on economic growth is generally a "new" approach in the smaller cities. One does not have to travel far to hear of plans by the retail merchants' association to keep out a chain store. Industrial

[14]Allison Davis, Burleigh B. Gardner, and Mary Gardner, *Deep South*, Chicago, University of Chicago Press, 1941, p. 255.

plants have been discouraged in city after city for fear that they would bring with them "undesirable" elements. Options on property are commonly utilized to prevent sale to outside interests. Local ordinances, such as the infamous Green River laws, are touted as protecting local citizens against unscrupulous door-to-door salesmen, although it is usually evident that the local retailers rather than local consumers are behind such proposals. How can such activities, many of which are extremely shortsighted, be carried out side-by-side with local pressures brought to bear on congressmen for an Air Force base or a bridge or dam, or the obviously eager industrial committee that baits its trap with careful location studies and promises of tax concessions?

To understand such apparent anomalies, one must consider the nature of the power structure in the community, the current economic base and its cultural implications, the nature of the importing or originating group, and a host of lesser factors. Obviously all towns and cities do not have the same sort of power structure. One of the important considerations, mentioned earlier, relates to the relative tightness of the power organization. Television and motion picture westerns depend heavily on the tightly organized power structure of the frontier town for their story lines. The large rancher, the banker, the saloon keeper, and the hotel owner (sometimes all the same individual) combine to run the town for their own purposes. The world of fiction normally errs in making the power group's plotting too overt, too venal, and too easily upset. In the small city dominated by a manufacturing family, a few financial and commercial interests, and a controlled political organization, neither the plot nor the characters are particularly simple. The people involved in the power structure are likely to be good citizens, supporting the churches, keeping the library and the hospital solvent, donating land for playgrounds, running the Community Chest or United Fund, and only incidentally discouraging a Chevrolet assembly plant or a Republic wire-rope operation.

The motivations of such groups are not obvious. But, in general, one can suggest certain tendencies. First, possessing power, but a rather feeble power compared with that of major national organizations, they are intent upon maintaining the local social organization with themselves as its leaders. Second, they usually have certain preconceptions about the kind of city they want theirs to be. Interested in economic development, they strongly prefer themselves to be the developers since this will result in an orderly process that will not get out of hand. But they are normally quite willing to encourage additional economic activities that are clean and do not threaten existing power relationships. High on the list of desirable institutions is the college or university, which requires few community services, maintains attractive surroundings, and is politically passive. By comparison, a manufacturing plant may entail growing union power (especially objectionable in those areas where industrial unions have small footholds), political unrest, the need for expensive community services, and the natural ugliness of many industrial installations. Further, if the proposed installation were that of a large corporation, the pure fear of facing a dominant economic power could be intense.

A small New England city with a local plant in receivership was faced with an offer to purchase from the Ford Motor Company. Henry Ford's known peculiarities and his great economic power prevented the purchase in spite of the acute economic need to get the plant in operation again. The local receivers saw a possible solution to the stalemate and suggested to the Ford negotiator that he quit his present job, take over the operation of the plant, and sell Ford the rolled copper in which he was interested. Of course, this meant that local financial sources had to put up additional funds since the negotiator had almost no capital for the operation. Ford accepted the proposal and agreed to purchase from the plant run by his former employee. The local power structure was quite pleased at solving a grave economic problem without becoming a "Ford" town.

Metropolitan Cities

In the larger, more cosmopolitan city there are likely to be fewer fears either of encroaching power or of changes in a way of life. The various power groups have learned in effect that it does not take 51 percent stock ownership to establish working control of a corporation or of anything else. A city like Atlanta casually changes its laws to accommodate Carling's without any particular fear that it may be "bad" for a town to have a brewery — despite the fact that Baptists and Methodists make up the two strongest church groups in the area. The sentimentality that characterizes the attachment of the power structure in smaller cities to traditional modes of behavior, its local landmarks, and its own individual members is generally missing in the metropolis. The president of a several-hundred-million dollar bank is less likely to be influenced by qualms about his in-group's possible relative loss of power than he is over the prospect of several hundred new depositors and borrowers. He has already learned that he cannot exert the power he has on all aspects of community life, and that he need not. There are presidents of other banks, large manufacturers, publishers, retailers, and the like who will indirectly watch out for his interests in activities he cannot attend to by himself or through a representative. In large part, this is simply the result of the major power groups having essentially the same interests rather than of their having a well-integrated or thoroughly spelled out program.

The reasons for the similarity of interests are not difficult to spell out. Business provides a major portion of the top leadership in the community.[15] This does not mean, of course, that businessmen always get their way or that they are always in agreement. Nor does it suggest that the interests of business are normally different from the interests of other elements of the community; the most spectacular examples of community economic development as a social process often indicate, as in the exclusion of railroads, a preoccupation with the maintenance of social order rather than with an increase in business profits. History seems to indicate that the existing power structure has always tended to identify social order with the maintenance of a contemporary social organization. For this reason, businessmen who are among the top community leaders are quite likely to have outlooks similar to those of others in positions of power. In fact, there is a considerable evidence that they are likely to be unimpressed by sheer wealth or social position and to accept as peers anyone who rises to a position of prominence. The result is that the power structure is usually but loosely related to the "society" groups of the area. Members of the local "400" are not necessarily in power positions, and many of those whose power is considerable may have small use for "all that social nonsense."

The power groups are, after all, involved in the management of a rather complex enterprise: the maintenance of a viable community. Their task is comparable to that of corporate management in maintaining a functioning organization. This entails numerous decisions

[15]See Robert S. Lynd and Helen Merrill Lynd, *Middletown in Transition*, New York, Harcourt, 1937; Floyd Hunter, *Community Power Structure*, Chapel Hill, University of North Carolina Press, 1953; or any of the numerous other community studies.

and activities that do not fall to any governmental body and for which there is no relevant formal organization. The informal power structure is the natural result. In a crude sense, the local Boy Scout organization, the United Fund, the municipal hospital, the Chamber of Commerce, the Optimist Club, even the local government can be thought of as working departments that carry out the policies of the power structure. A particularly explicit case is cited by Hunter.

"Charles Homer is the biggest man in our crowd. He gets an idea. When he gets an idea, others will get the idea. Don't ask me how he gets the idea or where. He may be in bed. He may think of it at breakfast. He may read a letter on the subject. But recently he got the idea that Regional City should be the national headquarters for an International Trade Council. He called in some of us (the inner crowd), and he talked briefly about his idea. He did not talk much. We do not engage in loose talk about the 'ideals' of the situation and all that other stuff. We get right down to the problem, that is, how to get this Council. We all think it is a good idea right around the circle. There are six of us in the meeting.

"All of us are assigned tasks to carry out. Moster is to draw up the papers of incorporation. He is the lawyer. I have a group of friends that I will carry along. Everyone else has a group of friends he will do the same with. These fellows are what you might call followers.

"We decide we need to raise $65,000 to put this thing over. We could raise that amount within our own crowd, but eventually this thing is going to be a community proposition, so we decide to bring the other crowds in on the deal. We decide to have a meeting at the Grandview Club with select members of other crowds.

"When we meet at the Club at Dinner with the other crowds, Mr. Homer makes a brief talk; again, he does not need to talk long. He ends his talk by saying he believes in his proposition enough that he is willing to put $10,000 of his own money into it for the first year. He sits down. You can see some of the other crowds getting their heads together, and the Growers Bank Crowd, not to be outdone, offers a like amount plus a guarantee that they will go along with the project for three years. Others throw in $5,000 to $10,000 until — I'd say within thirty or forty minutes — we have pledges of the money we need. In three hours the whole thing is settled, including the time for eating."

Mr. Treat paused for a moment, then continued: "There is one detail I left out, and it is an important one. We went into that meeting with a board of directors picked. The constitution was all written, and the man who was to head the council as executive was named — a fellow by the name of Lonny Dewberry, a third-string man, a fellow who will take advice."

The investigator asked how the public was apprised of the action. Mr. Treat said: "The public doesn't know anything about the project until it reaches the stage I've been talking about. After the matter is financially sound, then we go to the newspapers and say there is a proposal for consideration. Of course, it is not news to a lot of people by then, but the Chamber committees and other civic organizations are brought in on the idea. They all think it's a good idea. They held to get the Council located and established. That's about all there is to it."[16]

Of course, many decisions do not require any such careful preparation because the matters are relatively minor — they do not materially affect the interests of the power groups. A doctor in a small New England city wanted to sell a piece of property. The only problem in the sale was that the property was zoned as residential and the prospective purchaser wanted the land for commercial use. The doctor took his problem to the city clerk (whom he had delivered) to inquire about the difficulty of getting a change in zoning. It was soon determined that there was no particular reason why the change should not be made. In essence, this indicated that the doctor was much admired in the community and that no major power source would be inconvenienced by the change in zoning. The clerk did not have to clear this with anyone but could, from his knowledge of the local situation, predict the attitudes of various interests. He recommended that the doctor show up at the council meeting at which the matter would be decided. The doctor did, standing outside the chamber door for half an hour before the meeting and chatting with his friends on the council about the zoning change. During the meeting a group from one of the minority churches argued against the rezoning at length because their church was located near the doctor's land. They were listened to politely, then the rezoning was casually approved. In effect, activities of this sort depend on the relative power of groups and individuals rather more than they do to the economic consequences of the decision.

Social pressures of the same sort manifest themselves in even the simplest economic activity. They are often not apparent simply because there is no major social stake in the outcome. But when group loyalties or values are deeply involved, the social nature of what might appear to be purely economic behavior is clear.

[16]Floyd Hunter, *op. cit.*, pp. 173–174.

A realtor in a Southwestern city of moderate size was asked by one of the locally famous madams to sell both her place of business and her personal home. The realtor informed the madam that no real estate firm in the city would handle a former brothel, although the price was attractive. The madam advertised in the newspaper and sold the house in less than a week. Her personal home was another matter. The real estate firm was willing to handle this property for several reasons. Perhaps the most important of these was that the neighbors (among whom were counted both the mayor and a local minister) wanted to see the house sold. The personal home of the madam has not been sold at this writing after a year on the market. Obviously, from an economic standpoint it was a less desirable property to handle than the brothel. Socially, there is little question that it was more desirable to handle, especially since selling it would please some persons of moderate power.

It would be possible to cite an almost endless number of cases dealing with the various subtle and overt aspects of social relations that tend both to direct and to limit the economic development of communities of all sizes. They go far toward explaining why Milwaukee is a brewing town, why Thomasville became a clock center, why McCarthy built the Shamrock Hotel, why Kohler suffered a seven-year strike. They are important in understanding not only the major decisions involved in the location of a multimillion dollar plant but also the individual decisions by a dairy farmer to join DHIA or a real estate dealer to list a property.

Sometimes the decisions are wildly uneconomic, as was that of the Chamber of Commerce in Old City when it persuaded the new planing mill to reduce the wages it paid its largely Negro work force.[17] Wages that would have been spent in Old City were lowered 50 percent. But danger to the caste system, as seen by the Chamber of Commerce, was also reduced. Highly uneconomic activities of this sort generally imply the most intense social motivations.

In other cases the economic consequences are clearly favorable for the persons who push the program, as was the sale of a public beach in Salem for an electric power plant and a fuel dump.[18] But, in either case knowledge of the social motivations and the social mechanisms brought into play in the decision are necessary to an understanding of the event.

[17]Davis, Gardner, and Gardner, *op. cit.*, p. 261.
[18]Hunter, Schaffer, and Sheps, *op. cit.*, pp. 103–105.

11 ▶

Conclusions: A Theoretical Note

Economic theory and social theory are so different that it seems necessary to discuss, if only briefly, the nature of that difference before assessing the possibility of a real rapprochement between the two. Of course, it is not easy to summarize the nature of any sophisticated discipline without doing it at least some injustice. The attempt here is to point out what seem to be some of the critical differences between the disciplines of theoretical economics and of sociology without fully discussing or judging either.

Economic theory is long on assumptions and rigorous in its deductions of what must be the case, granting those assumptions. It tends to view an economy in terms of an input–output model of some sort and spends much of its effort determining how outputs are influenced by changing inputs. Further, it regards the outputs of one time period as the critical inputs of the next.

Social theory, on the other hand, is largely devoid of assumptions and might almost be regarded as a way of looking at things rather than as a theory. In so far as sociology does rest on assumptions, they are quite commonplace, apparently consisting first of the notion that if a person behaves in a particular way in a certain situation he will probably behave in much the same way in a similar situation. With this focus, it becomes necessary for the sociologist to spend much of his time comparing situations to determine what makes them similar and what does not. Second, sociology assumes that the more two people are alike in terms of such constructs as age, sex, culture, group affiliation, and class, the more probably they will behave in the same way.

It should be pointed out that sociologists take as a major portion of their task the testing of these assumptions by the collection of

150

empirical data, and that they are hindered in this process by the same inability to experiment that the economist suffers. The sociologist generally eschews the input–output model and favors situational analysis. And while he may on occasion predict human behavior from a knowledge of a situation, may even assume that elements of the situation unknown to him are "equal," he demands vastly more knowledge of the situation than the economist does knowledge of his inputs, which may be specified in simple quantitative terms. Beyond this, sociology remains largely qualitative in its description of behavior or situations, while economic theory is concerned largely with quantitative relationships. Lastly, economics is generally focused on cause-and-effect relationships, while sociology is more inclined to concern itself with sequences of behavior without the assumption of causality.

All of this sounds quite vague and not really to the point, because it lacks concreteness. What is really needed in order to understand the differences between the two disciplines is a discussion of the material of one in the terms of the other. For this purpose, I have chosen the first fully explicated economic proposition in a leading economic textbook of this period.[1] The reasons for choosing this example are that it is simple enough to comprehend without extensive background, typical of economic analysis, and stated with care by an individual whose abilities are nothing short of remarkable.

The proposition as stated by Samuelson is that societies must make a choice in the kinds of goods they desire to produce and that the nature of this choice can most clearly be seen by imagining a society that produced but two commodities: guns and butter. The alternative possibilities of the society are indicated by Table 2.

This table demonstrates one of the characteristics of choice quite clearly: no economy can produce the maximum of all its potential products. The resources used to produce butter can also be used to

TABLE 2

ALTERNATIVE POSSIBILITIES IN THE PRODUCTION OF GUNS AND BUTTER*

	A	B	C	D	E	F
Butter, millions of pounds	0	1	2	3	4	5
Guns, thousands	15	14	12	9	5	0

*After Samuelson, *op. cit.*, p. 18.

[1]Paul A. Samuelson, *Economics: An Introductory Analysis*, New York, McGraw-Hill, 1951, pp. 17–22.

produce guns; therefore, in producing any good the society is giving up the possibility of producing some other good with the same resources. The charting of these alternative possibilities shows another aspect of the relationship, delineated in Figure 1. The closer one gets to maximum gun production, the less efficient his transformation ratio. To produce the first five thousand guns requires that the economy forego one million pounds of butter; at higher levels of gun production an increase of a mere thousand (from fourteen thousand to fifteen thousand) requires the same amount of sacrifice in terms

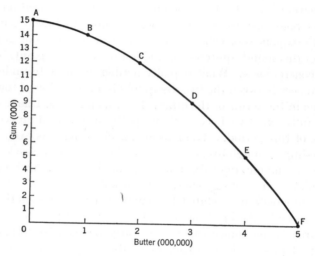

FIGURE 1. THIS CURVE, BASED ON THE POINTS INDICATED IN TABLE 1, SHOWS THE WAY IN WHICH INCREASING BUTTER PRODUCTION IMPLICATES DECREASING GUN PRODUCTION.

of butter. This is explained by the fact that the last resources to be allocated to gun production are not well adapted to that end, while the first to be allocated to it are.

The curve in Figure 1 is, of course, a full employment curve. With less than the full employment of resources, the points indicating production of guns and butter will lie inside the curve and will show that increased production of both guns and butter is possible.

The argument is straightforward and logical, given the assumptions of the economist, many of which are not stated. It is worth analyzing a few of these in the way a sociologist might — not to ridicule a brilliant economist but to demonstrate the different interests, methods, and assumptions of the two disciplines.

Before the sociologist would accept the curve as referring to some realistic statement of alternatives he would want to know a great deal about the people of the economy, their culture, their location, their present occupations, their social organization, and the physical world they inhabit. (Notice that the sociologist would be perfectly willing to discuss a gun–butter economy without quibbling over the obvious unrealities.) On the basis of the answers received, the sociologist would immediately point out that while some portions of the curve seemed to make sense, the whole curve simply could not stand — even as a theoretical structure. The reasons for this are relatively simple: an economy at point D (3,000,000 lb. of butter and 9,000 guns) simply could not convert to the production of guns only or butter only. Either of these alternatives would mean the relocation of workers from farm to factory or vice versa. Either would mean changing human values, changing social organizations and the like, and therefore be a process that would take decades. A more meaningful transformation curve for an economy at point D is given in Figure 2, and a transformation of even that magnitude could require a rather lengthy time.

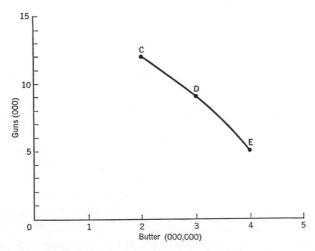

FIGURE 2. NOTE THAT THE SMALL SEGMENT OF THE CURVE WHICH RELATES TO A REALISTIC CHOICE MAY NOT HAVE MUCH "CURVE" LEFT IN IT.

The economist would naturally agree that no practical possibility of a major switch in production does exist — especially between two such dissimilar products as butter and guns. In all probability he would, however, point out that the concept is highly theoretical and that it does make sense to talk about the transformation curve as a set of "potential" choices which, if entered into freely by all members of the economy, would give the described result.

The sociologist, not averse to theoretical discussions, would undoubtedly answer that this is simply not the case. To suggest that all of the people in an economy enter into a single pursuit such as the production of guns only or butter only bespeaks a remarkably high morale and unity of opinion. Of course, if everyone entered into the plan there would be small problems at first, but the introduction of new persons with fresh ideas into the making of a single product and the fact that everyone would rapidly gain *expertise* so that talk everywhere would constantly revert to guns (or butter) would lead to rapid innovation in production methods. Therefore, the gun–butter transformation curve, based on high morale and innovation, should look like that in Figure 3.

FIGURE 3. SINCE NO SOCIOLOGIST WOULD PREDICT MORE THAN THE SHAPE OF THE CURVE, QUANTITIES HAVE NOT BEEN INDICATED ON EITHER AXIS.

The sociologist would know that the curve he drew was not really fair because it was based on a number of assumptions of his own, but he would argue violently that it was a possible transformation curve, given these assumptions.

At this point the economist would point out that he did not want to consider the vagaries of people. His original curve referred to a situation in which all the people of the economy were willing to undertake any task assigned and perform it with equal diligence, although their abilities might differ from task to task. Second, because he could see that the problem of transformation time was a major issue unless ruled out, he would also state as a requirement that the difference in transformation time from any point on the curve to any other point must be thought of as negligible.

Now let us take a look at the assumptions required for the serious consideration of the transformation curve:

1. The time required to shift from ond point on the transformation curve to any other point is identical, and none of these shifts take any longer than maintaining the relative production schedule that now exists.
2. The people of the society are essentially neutral, that is, they will take any job, accept any changing social forms required. They must be regarded as essentially the same bland and malleable stuff as other resources.

It would be ridiculous to jump to the conclusion that economic concepts lack power because their assumptions are either hidden or unrealistic. Different sorts of models like the transformation curve have different assumptions with different levels of sophistication and abstraction; the same assumptions do not carry throughout economic theory. In many cases assumptions about the nature of people (there is no single economic man) are based on compelling insights or evidence, although the assumptions are always relatively simple.

The nature of the economic discipline, then, is to make simplifying assumptions and to reason from these with great rigor. Progress within the history of economics has largely been related to the slow development of new and more contemporarily realistic assumptions and the remarkably thorough searching out of all the implications of these assumptions.

Sociology has worked the far end of the behavioral field, making a minimal number of assumptions. In fact, much progress in sociology (and the related study of anthropology) has been directed at the destruction of those few assumptions about people that have been long held. Margaret Mead's well-known New Guinea studies, for example, demonstrate that any inherent temperamental differences between the sexes are minimal.

Sociology is largely inductive, gathering great masses of data relating to the simplest kinds of human behavior and describing these with as few abstractions as possible. Its conclusions at present seem to be that human behavior can best be related to culture, class, and group and to the variables of age, sex, and position in the life cycle. With these constructs it can do a pretty good job of stating the alternative choices available to an individual and the relative likelihood of his choosing any one of them — so long as these are major lifetime choices rather than the relatively superficial choices of consumer economic behavior.

The purchase of a house might be the kind of economic decision or social behavior that either discipline could be expected to attack satisfactorily. The economist could predict quite well which of two houses would be purchased if all things other than price were equal. The sociologist could predict as well if everything but neighborhood were equal. But if the equality of other things could not be presumed, an experienced realtor might make a better prediction than either the economist or the sociologist — and none of the three would be highly reliable.

At the present time, the disciplines of sociology and economics have not reached far enough toward one another to make it mandatory that the theorist from either area consider the other as a portion of his *expertise*. But for this very reason the man of affairs, whether he be a businessman, economic policy advisor, or social planner, is under increasing pressure to become at least an informal student of both.

References

Ayers, C. E., *The Theory of Economic Progress*. Chapel Hill, University of North Carolina Press, 1944.

Bain, J. S., *Pricing, Distribution and Employment*. New York, Holt, 1953.

Caplow, Theodore, and Reece J. McGee, *Academic Market Place*. New York, Basic, 1958.

Cooley, Charles Horton, *Social Organization*. New York: Scribner, 1909.

Cyert, Richard M., and James G. March, *A Behavioral Theory of the Firm*. Englewood Cliffs, N. J., Prentice-Hall, 1963.

Davidson, Percy E., and H. Dewey Anderson, *Occupational Mobility in an American Community*. Stanford, Calif., Stanford University Press, 1937.

Davis, Allison, Burleigh B. Gardner, and Mary Gardner, *Deep South*. Chicago, University of Chicago Press, 1941.

Dollard, John, *Caste and Class in a Southern Town* (ed. 2). New York, Harper, 1949.

Dubin, Robert, *The World of Work*. Englewood Cliffs, N. J., Prentice-Hall, 1958.

Due, J. F., and R. W. Clower, *Intermediate Economic Analysis* (ed. 4). Homewood, Ill., Irwin, 1961.

Fayerweather, John, *Management of International Operations*. New York, McGraw-Hill, 1960.

Fenn, Dan H., Jr., *Management Guide to Overseas Operations*. New York, McGraw-Hill, 1957.

Frey, Albert Wesley, *How Many Dollars for Advertising?* New York, Ronald, 1955.

Gallaher, Art, Jr., *Plainville Fifteen Years Later*. New York, Columbia University Press, 1961.

Herskovits, Melville J., *Economic Anthropology*. New York, Knopf, 1952.

Hickerson, J. M., "Successful Sales Techniques," *Selling: Its Broader Dimensions* (Taylor W. Meloan and John M. Rathmell, Eds.). New York, Macmillan, 1960.

Homans, George C., *The Human Group*. New York, Harcourt, 1950.

157

Hunt, William Dudley, "Selling to One Group of Idealists — Architects," *Salesmanship: Modern Viewpoints on Personal Communication* (Steven J. Shaw and Joseph W. Thompson, Eds.). New York, Holt, 1960.

Hunter, Floyd, *Community Power Structure*. Chapel Hill, University of North Carolina Press, 1953.

Hunter, Floyd, Ruth C. Schaffer, and Cecil G. Sheps, *Community Organization: Action and Inaction*. Chapel Hill, University of North Carolina Press, 1956.

Katz, Elihu, and Paul F. Lazarsfeld, *Personal Influence*. New York, Free Press, 1955.

Kelley, Eugene J., "The Importance of Convenience in Consumer Purchasing," *Journal of Marketing*. Vol. 23, No. 1, Richard D. Irwin, Inc., Homewood, Ill., July 1958.

LaPiere, Richard, *A Theory of Social Control*. New York, McGraw-Hill, 1954.

Levine, Soloman B., *Industrial Relations in Postwar Japan*. Urbana, University of Illinois Press, 1950.

Lindzey, Gardner, Ed., "Man's Construction of His Alternatives," *The Assessment of Human Motives*. New York, Holt, 1958.

Lynd, Robert S., and Helen M. Lynd, *Middletown: A Study in Contemporary American Culture*. New York, Harcourt, 1929.

Lynd, Robert S., and Helen M. Lynd, *Middletown in Transition*. New York, Harcourt, 1937.

March, James G., and Herbert A. Simon, *Organization*. New York, Wiley, 1958.

Martineau, Pierre, "Social Class and Spending Behavior," *Salesmanship: Modern Viewpoints on Personal Communication* (Steven J. Shaw and Joseph W. Thompson, Eds.). New York, Holt, 1960.

Mills, C. Wright, *Power Elite*. New York, Oxford University Press, 1956.

Myrdal, Gunnar, *Rich Lands and Poor*. New York, Harper, 1957.

Packard, Vance, *Hidden Persuaders*. New York, McKay, 1957.

Rainwater, Lee, Richard P. Coleman, and Gerald Handel, *Workingman's Wife*. New York, Oceana, 1959.

Robinson, Richard D., *Cases in International Busine s*. New York, Holt, 1962.

Rogoff, Natalie, *Recent Trends in Occupational Mobility*. New York, Free Press, 1953.

Roth, Charles B., *My Lifetime Treasury of Selling Secrets*. Englewood Cliffs, N. J., Prentice-Hall, 1957.

Rucker, Cason, "Basic Selling," *Selling: Its Broader Dimensions* (Taylor W. Meloan and John M. Rathmell, Eds.). New York, Macmillan, 1960.

Samuelson, Paul A., *Economics: An Introductory Analysis*. New York, McGraw-Hill, 1951.

Sargent, Hugh, *Consumer-Product Rating Publications and Buying Behavior*. Urbana, Ill., Bureau of Business and Economic Research, University of Illinois, 1959.

Shister, Joseph, *Economics of the Labor Market*. Philadelphia, Lippincott, 1956.

Sievers, Allen M., *Revolution, Evolution and the Economic Order*. Englewood Cliffs, N. J., Prentice-Hall, 1962.

Simon, Herbert A., *Administrative Behavior* (2nd ed.). New York, Macmillan, 1961.

Stigler, G. J., *The Theory of Price* (rev. ed.). New York: Macmillan, 1952.

Thompson, Virginia, *Labor Problems in Southeast Asia*. New Haven, Yale University Press, 1947.

Tucker, W. T., *Advertising Appropriations Methods in Banking*. Atlanta, Georgia State College Bureau of Business and Economic Research, 1959.

Warner, W. Lloyd, and James C. Abegglen, *Occupational Mobility in American Business and Industry*. Minneapolis, University of Minnesota Press, 1955.

Warner, W. Lloyd, and J. O. Low, *The Social System of the Modern Factory*. New Haven, Yale University Press, 1947.

Warner, W. Lloyd, and Paul S. Lunt, *The Status System of a Modern Community* (Vol. II, Yankee City Series). New Haven, Yale University Press, 1942.

Warner, W. Lloyd, M. Meeker, and K. Eells, *Social Class in America*. Chicago, Science Research Associates, 1949.

Weale, W. Bruce, "Are We Good Enough for Your Product?" *Salesmanship: Modern Viewpoints on Personal Communication* (Steven J. Shaw and Joseph W. Thompson, Eds.). New York, Holt, 1960.

West, James, *Plainville, U.S.A.* New York, Columbia University Press, 1945.

Whyte, William Foote, *Money and Motivation*. New York, Harper, 1955.

Whyte, William Foote, *Men at Work*. Homewood, Ill., Dorsey, 1961.

Williams, Robin M., Jr., *American Society, A Sociological Interpretation* (ed. 2). New York, Knopf, 1960.

Zimmermann, Eric W., *World Resources and Industries* (rev. ed.). New York, Harper, 1951.

Zipf, George Kingsley, *Human Behavior and the Principle of Least Effort*. Reading, Mass., Addison-Wesley, 1949.

Index

Abegglen, James C., 54n.
Advertising appropriation, an organizational decision, 114–124
  factors that influence, 121–124
  formal methods, 118–121
  rational approach to, 115–117
Anderson, H. Dewey, 54
Ayers, C. E., 137

Bain, J. S., 2n.
Barriers to trade, cultural (international business), 125–127
Birdseye, Clarence, 137
Business organization, nature of the, 93–113
  corporate decisions, context of, 108–113
  formal and informal, 97–100
  goals, corporate and personal, 94–97
  loyalty, references of, 104–108
  power, disposition of, 100–104
Business sales, sociology of, 81–87
  see also Sale, the
Buyer-seller relationship, 70–73

Caplow, Theodore, 58
Career choice, 50–58
Cities, metropolitan, economic development, 145–149

Clark, J. M., 2
Class, 14–18
  consumer and, 41–45
Clower, R. W., 2n.
Coleman, Richard P., 43n.
Community economic development, 136–149
  hierarchic communities, 142–145
  metropolitan cities, 145–149
  primitive, 137–138
  small community, the, 139–142
Company loyalty, 106
Consumer, the, 28–49
  class and, 41–45
  culture and, 35–41
  group and, 45–49
  subgoals, economic, 33–35
Cooley, Charles Horton, 11
Corporate decisions, context of, 108–113
  advertising appropriation, 114–124
Corporate goals, personal and, 94–97
Culture, 22–24
  businessman as missionary of, 134–135
  consumer and, 35–41
  trade barriers, international business, 125–127
  see also Subcultures

Cyert, Richard M., 94n.

Davidson, Percy E., 54
Davis, Allison, 143n., 149n.
Decisions
  corporate, context of, 108–113
    advertising appropriation, 114–124
  economic, variety in, 25–27
Departmental loyalty, 105–106
Development, economic community,
  see Community economic develop-
  ment
Dollard, John, 15n.
Door-to-door selling, 79–80
Dubin, Robert, 59n., 104, 112
Due, J. F., 2n.

Economic theory, 2, 96n., 150–156
Eells, K., 15n.
Ethnocentrism, 126
European Common Market, 126
Events, economic, nature of, 4–13

Fayerweather, John, 133, 134
Ford, Henry, 145
Ford, Henry, II, 16
Foreign markets, adapting to, 128–129
Forester, E. M., 126
Formal business organization, 97–100
Frey, Albert Wesley, 119n.

Galbraith, J. K., 2
Gallaher, Art, Jr., 139n., 140–141
Gardner, Burleigh B., 143n., 149n.
Gardner, Mary, 143n., 149n.
Getty, J. Paul, 16
Goals, *see* Corporate goals; Occupa-
  tional goals; Personal goals; Sub-
  goals
Goldwater, Barry, 15, 16
Goldwyn, Sam, 16
Group, the, 18–22
  consumer and, 45–49

Handel, Gerald, 43
Hart, A. S., 128
Hawley, Cameron, 86
Herskovits, Melville J., 129, 130
Hickerson, J. M., 83n.

Homans, George C., 22n.
Hunt, William Dudley, 82n.
Hunter, Floyd, 142n., 146n., 147–148,
  149n.

Incentive pay, 62–63
Informal business organization, 97–100
Institution, defined, 19
International business, 125–135
  cultural barriers to trade, 125–127
  cultural missionary, businessman as,
    134–135
  foreign markets, adapting to, 128–129
  overseas production, 130–134
Interview for job, 55–58

Job interview, 55–58
Job satisfaction, 61–62
  work behavior and, 62–65

Katz, Elihu, 46
Kelley, Eugene J., 34
Kelly, George A., 7n.
Kennedy, John F., 16

Lane, Mills B., 124
Lanza, Mario, 128
LaPiere, Richard, 19n.
Lazarsfeld, Paul F., 46
Least effort, principle of, 8
Lee, Robert E., 33
Levine, Solomon B., 132n.
Limited use, concept of, 9
Lodge, Henry Cabot, 16
Low, J. O., 111
Loyalty, references of, business organi-
  zation, 104–108
Lunt, Paul S., 15n.
Lynd, Robert S., and Helen M., 15n.,
  146n.

McGee, Reece J., 58
March, James G., 63n., 94n., 104
Marginal utility, 9, 10
Markets, foreign, adapting to, 128–129
Marshall, Alfred, 2
Martineau, Pierre, 74
Mead, Margaret, 156
Meeker, M., 15n.

Metropolitan cities, economic development, 145–149
Mills, C. Wright, 58
Mitford, Nancy, 15
Mobility, work and, 65–68
Motivation, 7–13
Myrdal, Gunnar, 135

Occupational goals, 50–52
Organization, business, *see* Business organization
Organization slack, concept of, 94n.
Overseas production, 130–134

Packard, Vance, 28n.
Paternalism, 132–133
Personal goals, corporate and, 94–97
Piece-work rates, 63–64
Power, disposition of, business organization, 100–104
Price theory, 2
Primitive community development, 137–138
Professional loyalty, 106–107
Promotion system, 112
Protocols, hierarchic, 88–92

Rainwater, Lee, 43
Retail sales, sociology of, 73–81
Reward for work, 59–62
Robinson, Richard D., 126, 132n.
Rogoff, Natalie, 54n.
Roth, Charles, 71
Rucker, Cason, 83n.

Salaries and wages, 61–64, 111–112
Sale, the, 69–92
    business, sociology of, 81–87
    buyer-seller relationship, 70–73
    hierarchic protocols, 88–92
    retail, sociology of, 73–81
Samuelson, Paul A., 151
Sargent, Hugh, 47
Satisficing, concept of, 9–10
Schafer, Harold, 82–83
Schaffer, Ruth C., 142n., 149n.

Schumpter, J. A., 2
Seli, Kemal, 132
Sheps, Cecil G., 142n., 149n.
Shister, Joseph, 54n.
Sievers, Allen M., 113n.
Simon, Herbert A., 63n., 98n., 104
Small community economic development, 139–142
Smith, Adam, 2
Snow, C. P., 86
Social theory, 10–13, 150–156
Stanley Home Products, 80
Status demands, 64–65
Stigler, G. J., 2n.
Subcultures, 38–39
Subgoals, economic, 33–35

Thompson, Virginia, 132, 134–135
Trade, cultural barriers to, 125–127
Tucker, W. T., 115n., 117n.

Veblen, Thorstein, 2, 24, 61

Wages and salaries, 61–64, 111–112
Wants, 30–32
Warner, W. Lloyd, 15, 54n., 111
Weale, Bruce, 43
West, James, 15n., 139, 140, 141
Whyte, William Foote, 59n., 63n., 65–66, 95, 111
Williams, Robin M., Jr., 15
Willkie, Wendell, 112–113
Wilson, Charles, 104
Work, 50–68
    career choice, 50–58
    job satisfaction, work behavior and, 62–65
    mobility and, 65–68
    rewards for, 59–62
Work behavior, job satisfaction and, 62–65
Work-group loyalty, 105

Zimmermann, Eric W., 136
Zipf, George Kingsley, 8